D1309170

Family Circle.

Quick & Easy
Cooking

Meredith₊ Consumer Marketing
Des Moines, Iowa

Family Circle® Quick & Easy Cooking

Meredith® Corporation Consumer Marketing
Vice President, Consumer Marketing: Janet Donnelly
Consumer Product Marketing Director: Heather Sorensen
Business Director: Ron Clingman
Consumer Marketing Product Manager: Wendy Merical
Senior Production Manager: Al Rodruck

Waterbury Publications, Inc.
Editorial Director: Lisa Kingsley
Associate Editor: Tricia Bergman
Creative Director: Ken Carlson
Associate Design Director: Doug Samuelson
Graphic Designer: Mindy Samuelson
Contributing Copy Editor: Terri Fredrickson
Contributing Proofreader: Peg Smith
Contributing Indexer: Elizabeth T. Parson

Family Circle® **Magazine**
Editor in Chief: Linda Fears
Creative Director: Karmen Lizzul
Food Director: Regina Ragone, M.S., R.D.
Senior Food Editor: Julie Miltenberger
Associate Food Editor: Michael Tyrrell

Meredith Publishing Group
President: Tom Harty

Meredith Corporation
President and Chief Executive Officer: Stephen M. Lacy

In Memoriam: E.T. Meredith III (1933–2003)

Pictured on the front cover:
Carolina Pulled Pork
(recipe page 222)

Copyright © 2012 by
Meredith Corporation.
Des Moines, Iowa.
First Edition.
Printed in the United States of America.
ISSN: 1942-7468
ISBN: 978-0-696-30133-9
All of us at Meredith® Consumer Marketing are
dedicated to providing you with information
and ideas to enhance your home. We welcome
your comments and suggestions. Write to us at:
Meredith Consumer Marketing, 1716 Locust St.,
Des Moines, IA 50309-3023.

Night after night and bite after bite, families agree that nothing beats fresh home-cooked meals. Busy cooks who pull off the dinnertime challenge with ease admit that some of their best, most requested family meals require only a handful of ingredients and a couple of easy steps. They favor no-fuss recipes like these as they continue to look for ways to minimize the stress of family mealtime.

Thumb through the pages of *Quick and Easy Cooking* and discover some of the slickest ways to throw together dinner, even on the days when you have little time or energy to cook a hot meal. This book is bursting with recipes, including easy, versatile pastas, quick-to-grill meats, toss-and-serve salads, and fix-and-forget slow-cooker meals. Recipe ingredient lists specify the familiar basics at any supermarket—fresh and prepared foods as well as convenience items. Along with that, nearly all of these recipes have the cook out of the kitchen in fewer than 30 minutes.

One of the best ways to experience the convenience of this book is to spend a few minutes on a weekend selecting recipes for the upcoming week. Write menus, do the shopping, and stick the menu list on the fridge. Check it throughout the week to jog your memory for important steps, such as thawing meat or allowing time in the morning to put ingredients in a slow cooker. The more you plan, the easier it becomes to whip together a weeknight meal, come to the table with a smile, and say, "Dinner is served!"

Because health and time-saving features are paramount these days, look for the following icons throughout the book:

 Healthy: The "healthy" icon means that the recipe meets certain calorie, fat, and sodium guidelines. See page 336 for more information.

 One-Pan: The "one-pan" icon means that the recipe uses a single pan in its preparation, and that translates to easy cleanup.

TABLE OF CONTENTS

47   110   252

321

Beef, pork, and lamb assure hearty, satisfying fare. Whether you plan a special dinner or a quick meal on a busy weeknight, look here for an array of recipes that are sure to become favorites.

15

20

31

MEATY MAIN DISHES

48

Beef and Baby Spuds with Tomato-Olive Ragoût

Serve this meat-and-potatoes meal with a simple arugula salad. Dress the greens with a splash of fresh lemon juice, olive oil, salt, and pepper—then top them off with a little shaved Parmesan.

MAKES 4 servings **START TO FINISH** 25 minutes

- 1 pound baby Yukon gold or new potatoes, halved and/or quartered
- 4 teaspoons olive oil
- 4 4-ounce beef steaks cut ½ inch thick (flat iron, strip, sirloin, or rib eye)
- 8 ounces cherry tomatoes
- 3 cloves garlic, sliced
- ¾ cup pitted green olives, coarsely chopped
- 1 teaspoon snipped fresh oregano or ½ teaspoon dried

① Cook potatoes, covered with vented plastic wrap, in microwave-safe bowl for 5 minutes, stirring once.

② Meanwhile, season steaks with salt and pepper. Heat a large skillet over medium-high heat; add 1 teaspoon of the olive oil. Cook steaks 3 to 4 minutes per side. Transfer to platter; cover. In same skillet cook tomatoes and garlic in the remaining 1 teaspoon oil until softened. Stir in olives and oregano; cook 3 minutes more.

③ In separate nonstick skillet cook potatoes in 2 teaspoons hot oil for 4 minutes over medium-high heat. Season with salt and pepper. Serve steaks and potatoes with sauce.

PER SERVING 409 cal, 23 g fat (7 g sat. fat), 53 mg chol, 643 mg sodium, 24 g carb, 4 g fiber, 26 g pro

quick tip Flat-iron steak (also called top blade steak) is a relatively new cut that has become very popular with steak lovers the past few years. Cut from the shoulder of beef, it offers rich flavor and tender texture for a good price. It's so named because its flat shape recalls that of an old-fashioned metal flat iron.

Italian Fried Steak with Roasted Pepper Pesto

This fresh and contemporary take on classic Italian pepper steak is elegant enough to serve to company.

MAKES 4 servings **START TO FINISH** 30 minutes

- ½ cup seasoned fine dry bread crumbs
- ½ cup grated Romano or Parmesan cheese
- 1 egg
- 2 tablespoons water
- 1½ pounds beef cubed steak
  Olive oil
- 1 12-ounce jar roasted red sweet peppers, drained
- ⅔ cup fresh basil leaves

① In a shallow dish combine crumbs and half the cheese. In another shallow dish beat together egg and the water. Cut meat in 8 equal-size portions; lightly sprinkle with salt and pepper. Dip in egg mixture, then crumb mixture; press lightly to coat.

② In a large skillet heat 1 tablespoon olive oil over medium-high heat. Working in two batches, cook steak, about 5 minutes per side, adding more oil as needed. Transfer to a serving platter; cover to keep warm. Carefully wipe skillet clean.

③ Meanwhile, for sauce, in blender or processor combine drained peppers and remaining cheese. Process until nearly smooth. Finely chop ½ cup of the basil; set aside. Transfer sauce to hot skillet and heat through. Remove from heat. Stir in finely chopped basil. Pour sauce over steaks. Sprinkle with remaining basil.

PER SERVING 425 cal, 21 g fat (8 g sat. fat), 130 mg chol, 645 mg sodium, 15 g carb, 2 g fiber, 43 g pro

Beef and Baby Spuds with
Tomato-Olive Ragoût

Wine-Glazed Steak

Wine-Glazed Steak

This sirloin steak owes its bold flavor to a tantalizing mix of red wine, balsamic vinegar, soy sauce, and honey.

MAKES 2 servings **START TO FINISH** 30 minutes

1	boneless beef top sirloin steak, cut ½ to ¾ inch thick (8 to 10 ounces total)
2	teaspoons olive oil
1	cup sliced fresh mushrooms
2	cloves garlic, minced
⅛	teaspoon crushed red pepper
¼	cup dry red wine or low-calorie cranberry juice*
2	tablespoons balsamic vinegar
1	tablespoon reduced-sodium soy sauce
1	teaspoon honey*

① Trim fat from steak; cut steak into two equal portions. In a large skillet heat oil over medium-high heat. Add steaks. Reduce heat to medium; cook for 10 to 13 minutes or until desired doneness (145°F for medium-rare or 160°F for medium doneness), turning steaks occasionally. If steaks brown too quickly, reduce heat to medium-low. Transfer steaks to a serving platter; keep warm.

② Add mushrooms, garlic, and crushed red pepper to skillet; cook and stir for 2 minutes. Remove skillet from heat. Carefully add wine. Return to heat. Boil gently, uncovered, for 3 to 5 minutes or until most of the liquid is evaporated. Add balsamic vinegar, soy sauce, and honey; return to simmering. Cook and stir about 2 minutes or until slightly thickened. Spoon over steaks.

PER SERVING 267 cal, 9 g fat (2 g sat. fat), 48 mg chol, 336 mg sodium, 11 g carb, 1 g fiber, 28 g pro

*NOTE If using the cranberry juice option, omit the honey.

Beef and Noodle Toss

If you don't have lasagna noodles, extra-wide egg noodles —left whole—would work equally well.

MAKES 4 servings **START TO FINISH** 25 minutes

8	ounces lasagna noodles
12	ounces boneless beef sirloin, cut into bite-size pieces
½	teaspoon salt
½	teaspoon black pepper
2	tablespoons all-purpose flour
1	tablespoon olive oil
1	pint grape tomatoes (2 cups)
8	ounces sliced cremini or button mushrooms
4	cloves garlic, minced (2 teaspoons)
1	14.5-ounce can beef broth

① Break noodles in half; cook according to package directions. Drain (do not rinse).

② Meanwhile; season beef with salt and pepper. Toss with flour. Heat oil in a large skillet over medium-high heat. Add meat, any remaining flour, and the tomatoes to skillet. Cook 3 to 4 minutes or until beef is well browned, stirring often. Add mushrooms and garlic. Cook 5 minutes more. Add broth; cook 3 to 4 minutes or until beef is done and liquid is slightly thickened.

③ Add cooked noodles to skillet; stir gently to coat. Heat through. Spoon into pasta bowls to serve.

PER SERVING 468 cal, 16 g fat (5 g sat. fat), 40 mg chol, 712 mg sodium, 52 g carb, 3 g fiber, 28 g pro

《 No matter how simple and quick the recipe, a steak dinner conveys a sense of specialness to the evening. 》

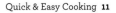

Beef Tips with Cornichons ☕

For something a little more interesting than hot cooked noodles or rice, serve this saucy beef dish over hot cooked spaetzle—small German dumplings.

MAKES 4 servings **START TO FINISH** 35 minutes

- 1 tablespoon cooking oil
- ½ cup chopped onion
- 1 teaspoon bottled minced garlic (2 cloves)
- ¼ cup dry white wine
- 1 17-ounce package refrigerated cooked beef tips with gravy
- ⅓ cup cornichons, sliced lengthwise (see quick tip, below)
- ½ teaspoon dried tarragon, crushed
- ½ cup sour cream
  Hot cooked noodles or rice

① In a large skillet heat oil over medium heat. Add onion and garlic; cook and stir until onion is tender. Add white wine. Bring to boiling; reduce heat. Simmer, uncovered, until reduced by half.

② Add beef tips with gravy, cornichons, and tarragon to skillet; cook until heated through. Stir in sour cream. Serve immediately over hot cooked noodles or rice.

PER SERVING 347 cal, 16 g fat (6 g sat. fat), 84 mg chol, 828 mg sodium, 28 g carb, 2 g fiber, 22 g pro

quick tip Look for the small sweet-sour French pickles called cornichons with other pickles at supermarkets or food specialty stores.

Beef with Mushrooms and Pearl Onions in Red Wine Reduction ☕ ♥

A reduction is a simple sauce made by boiling off the water in broth and/or wine. As the liquid reduces and the water boils off, flavors become more concentrated.

MAKES 4 servings **START TO FINISH** 30 minutes

- 2 8-ounce beef top loin steaks, cut ¾ to 1 inch thick
- ½ teaspoon cracked black pepper
- ¼ teaspoon salt
- 1 teaspoon olive oil
- 8 ounces fresh mushrooms, quartered
- 1 cup frozen small whole onions
- 4 cloves garlic, minced
- ¾ cup dry red wine
- 1 cup lower-sodium beef broth
- 2 tablespoons whole wheat flour
- 1 tablespoon snipped fresh parsley
  Steamed green beans and/or crusty whole grain bread (optional)

① Trim fat from steaks. Sprinkle steaks with pepper and salt. Preheat a large skillet over medium-high heat. Add oil; swirl to lightly coat skillet. Reduce heat to medium. Add steaks; cook for 8 minutes for medium-rare (145°F) or 10 minutes for medium (160°F), turning once halfway through cooking. Transfer steaks to a tray or plate; cover with foil and let stand while preparing sauce.

② For the sauce, in the same skillet cook mushrooms and onions over medium-high heat about 5 minutes or until tender, stirring frequently. Add garlic. Cook for 1 minute more. Remove skillet from heat; add wine. Return skillet to heat. Boil gently, uncovered, for 5 minutes, stirring occasionally. Whisk together broth and flour; add to skillet. Cook and stir until sauce is thickened and bubbly; cook and stir for 1 minute more.

③ Return steaks to skillet; heat through, turning to coat steaks evenly with sauce. Transfer steaks and sauce to serving plates. Sprinkle with parsley. If desired, serve with green beans and/or whole grain bread.

PER SERVING 335 cal, 17 g fat (6 g sat. fat), 61 mg chol, 315 mg sodium, 9 g carb, 2 g fiber, 26 g pro

Beef with Mushrooms and
Pearl Onions in Red Wine Reduction

Seared Beef with Orange Salsa

Seared Beef with Orange Salsa

Use a mortar and pestle to crush the fennel seeds and black peppercorns.

MAKES 4 servings **START TO FINISH** 30 minutes

4	large oranges
2	teaspoons fennel seeds, crushed
2	teaspoons black peppercorns, crushed
¼	teaspoon kosher salt
12	ounces beef tenderloin, cut into 4 steaks (each about ¾ inch thick)
1	tablespoon olive oil
½	cup finely chopped red onion
¼	cup pitted kalamata olives, quartered
¼	cup chopped fresh parsley leaves
2	tablespoons lemon juice
2	tablespoons olive oil
1	clove garlic, finely chopped
½	teaspoon paprika
4	cups torn arugula leaves

① Finely shred orange peel to equal 2 teaspoons. In a small bowl combine orange peel, fennel seeds, peppercorns, and salt. Sprinkle evenly over beef.

② In a large skillet heat 1 tablespoon oil over medium-high heat; add the meat. Reduce heat to medium. Cook for 7 minutes until medium-rare (145°F) or 9 minutes for medium (160°F), turning once halfway through cooking. Slice meat across the grain in thin slices.

③ Meanwhile, peel and section oranges. In a large bowl combine orange sections, red onion, olives, parsley, lemon juice, 2 tablespoons olive oil, the garlic, and paprika. Stir gently to combine.

④ Add arugula to orange mixture; toss to combine. Divide arugula mixture among 4 dinner plates. Serve with sliced meat.

PER SERVING 318 cal, 18 g fat (4 g sat. fat), 52 mg chol, 263 mg sodium, 21 g carb, 5 g fiber, 20 g pro

Espresso-Rubbed Steak with Green Chile Pesto

Use Anaheim or poblano chiles in the Green Chile Pesto. Both are fairly mild varieties—they simply add a fresh chile taste to the gorgeous green sauce.

MAKES 8 servings **START TO FINISH** 30 minutes

1½	pounds beef flank steak
2	teaspoons chili powder
1	teaspoon kosher salt or ½ teaspoon regular salt
1	teaspoon instant espresso coffee powder
½	teaspoon garlic powder
½	teaspoon dried oregano, crushed
½	teaspoon black pepper
	Nonstick cooking spray
1	recipe Green Chile Pesto

① Trim fat from steak. Score both sides of steak in a diamond pattern by making shallow diagonal cuts at 1-inch intervals. In a small bowl stir together chili powder, salt, espresso powder, garlic powder, oregano, and pepper. Sprinkle chili powder mixture evenly over steak; rub in with your fingers.

② Coat an large unheated nonstick skillet with cooking spray. Heat over medium-high heat; add steak. Reduce heat to medium. Cook for 12 to 14 minutes for medium-rare (145°F) or 14 to 16 minutes for medium (160°F), turning once halfway through cooking. Transfer to a cutting board. Cover with foil; let stand for 10 minutes before slicing.

③ Meanwhile, prepare the Green Chile Pesto. To serve, thinly slice steak against grain. Pass Green Chile Pesto.

Green Chile Pesto: Halve 2 medium fresh Anaheim or poblano chile peppers lengthwise; remove stems, seeds, and veins (see note, page 47). Coarsely chop peppers. In a food processor combine peppers, ½ cup fresh cilantro leaves, ¼ cup crumbled Cotija cheese, 2 tablespoons pine nuts, 2 cloves garlic, ¼ teaspoon crushed red pepper, dash salt, and dash black pepper. Cover and process to finely chop. With processor running, add ⅓ cup olive oil in a steady stream through feed tube; process to a coarse paste.

PER SERVING 244 cal, 17 g fat (3 g sat. fat), 31 mg chol, 335 mg sodium, 4 g carb, 1 g fiber, 20 g pro

Fajita-Style Beef Tacos

Ripe mango offers a fresh and sweet touch to these hearty beef tacos.

MAKES 4 servings **PREP** 15 minutes
BROIL 8 minutes **STAND** 5 minutes

- 12 ounces boneless beef sirloin steak, cut ¾ inch thick
- ⅛ teaspoon salt
- ⅛ teaspoon black pepper
- ⅛ teaspoon cayenne pepper
- 1 tablespoon canola oil
- 2 cups halved and thinly sliced sweet onions, such as Vidalia or Maui
- 1 mango, seeded, peeled, and chopped
- 8 6-inch corn tortillas, warmed
- ¼ cup snipped fresh cilantro
  Lime wedges

① Preheat broiler. Trim fat from steak. In a small bowl combine salt, black pepper, and cayenne pepper; sprinkle evenly over steak. Place steak on the unheated rack of a broiler pan. Broil 3 to 4 inches from the heat for 8 minutes for medium-rare (145°F) or 10 minutes for medium (160°F), turning once halfway through cooking. Cover with foil; let steak stand for 5 minutes.

② Meanwhile, in a large skillet heat oil over medium heat. Add onions; cover and cook about 12 minutes or until very tender and brown, stirring occasionally. Reduce heat to medium-low if onions start to get too brown.

③ Thinly slice steak across the grain. Divide steak, onions, and mango among tortillas. Sprinkle each with cilantro and serve with lime wedges for squeezing. Serve immediately.

PER SERVING 377 cal, 15 g fat (5 g sat. fat), 39 mg chol, 140 mg sodium, 41 g carb, 6 g fiber, 22 g pro

Tenderloins with Rosemary and Mushrooms 🍲 ♥

Serve this steakhouse-style entrée with mashed potatoes and spinach sautéed in garlic.

MAKES 4 servings **PREP** 15 minutes **COOK** 15 minutes

- 1 tablespoon butter
- 1 tablespoon cooking oil
- 4 beef tenderloin steaks, cut 1 inch thick
- 2 cups sliced fresh mushrooms
- ¼ cup sliced green onion
- 1 tablespoon snipped fresh rosemary or 1 teaspoon dried rosemary, crushed
- ½ teaspoon bottled minced garlic (1 clove)
- ¼ teaspoon black pepper
- ⅓ cup dry sherry, dry red wine, or beef broth
  Fresh rosemary sprigs (optional)

① Trim fat from steaks. In large skillet heat butter and oil over medium-high heat. Add steaks; reduce heat to medium. Cook for 10 minutes for medium-rare (145°F) or 13 minutes for medium (160°F), turning once halfway through cooking. Transfer steaks to serving platter, reserving drippings in skillet. Cover steaks; keep warm.

② Stir mushrooms, green onion, the snipped or dried rosemary, garlic, and pepper into reserved drippings. Cook and stir over medium-high heat for 3 to 4 minutes or until mushrooms are tender. Reduce heat. Carefully stir in sherry.

③ Cook and stir about 1 minute more or until heated through. Serve steaks with mushrooms. If desired, garnish with fresh rosemary sprigs.

PER SERVING 249 cal, 14 g fat (4 g sat. fat), 64 mg chol, 83 mg sodium, 4 g carb, 1 g fiber, 23 g pro

Frizzled Eggs over Garlic Steak
and Mushroom Hash

Frizzled Eggs over Garlic Steak and Mushroom Hash 🍲 ♥

What's a "frizzled" egg? An egg that has been cracked into a very hot skillet so the edges of the white become delightfully crispy.

MAKES 4 servings **START TO FINISH** 30 minutes

- 2 tablespoons vegetable oil
- 2 cups frozen diced hash brown potatoes with onions and peppers
- 1 8-ounce package sliced fresh mushrooms
- 4 3-ounce thin breakfast steaks
- 4 cloves garlic, thinly sliced
- 4 eggs
  Fresh tarragon (optional)

① In a large skillet heat 1 tablespoon of the oil. Cook potatoes and mushrooms, covered, over medium-high heat for 10 minutes. Stir occasionally. Remove from skillet; cover to keep warm.

② Sprinkle steaks with salt and pepper. Heat remaining oil in skillet. Cook steaks and garlic for 3 to 4 minutes for medium-rare (145°F), turning once halfway through cooking. Remove from skillet; cover to keep warm.

③ Add each egg to the hot skillet; sprinkle salt and pepper. Cook to desired doneness. Place potatoes, steaks, and eggs on plates. If desired sprinkle fresh tarragon.

PER SERVING 324 cal, 15 g fat (3 g sat. fat), 258 mg chol, 397 mg sodium, 17 g carb, 2 g fiber, 29 g pro

Five-Spice Steak Wraps

Five-Spice Steak Wraps ♥

Five-spice powder is a Chinese spice blend made from cinnamon, cloves, fennel seed, star anise, and Szechuan peppercorns.

MAKES 4 servings **START TO FINISH** 25 minutes

- 12 ounces boneless beef round steak
- 2 cups packaged shredded cabbage with carrot (coleslaw mix)
- ¼ cup red and/or green sweet pepper, cut into thin bite-size strips
- ¼ cup julienned carrot
- ¼ cup snipped fresh chives
- 2 tablespoons rice vinegar
- ½ teaspoon toasted sesame oil
- ½ teaspoon five-spice powder
- ¼ teaspoon salt
  Nonstick cooking spray
- ¼ cup plain low-fat yogurt or light sour cream
- 4 8-inch flour tortillas

① If desired, partially freeze steak for easier slicing. In a medium bowl combine coleslaw mix, sweet pepper, carrot, and chives. In a small bowl combine vinegar and sesame oil. Pour over coleslaw; toss to coat. Set aside.

② Trim fat from steak. Thinly slice steak across the grain into ¼-inch-thick strips. Sprinkle steak with five-spice powder and salt. Coat an unheated medium nonstick skillet with nonstick cooking spray. Preheat skillet over medium-high heat. Add steak strips; stir-fry for 3 to 4 minutes or until brown.

③ To assemble, spread 1 tablespoon of the yogurt in the center of each tortilla. Top with steak strips. Stir coleslaw; spoon over steak. Roll tortillas. If desired, secure with wooden toothpicks.

PER SERVING 237 cal, 7 g fat (2 g sat. fat), 51 mg chol, 329 mg sodium, 20 g carb, 2 g fiber, 22 g pro

Beef, Mushroom, and Onion Tart

Serve squares of this beefy, cheesy tart with a crisp green salad.

MAKES 4 servings **START TO FINISH** 30 minutes
OVEN 425°F

- 12 ounces lean ground beef
- 1 8-ounce package sliced mushrooms
- ½ of a medium red onion, cut in thin wedges
- ¼ teaspoon salt
- ¼ teaspoon black pepper
- 1 13- to 14-ounce package refrigerated pizza dough
- 3 ounces blue cheese, crumbled

  Fresh oregano and/or pizza seasoning (optional)

① Heat oven to 425°F. In a large skillet cook beef, mushrooms, and onion over medium heat about 8 minutes or until beef is browned and onion is tender, stirring occasionally. Drain off fat. Stir in salt and pepper.

② Meanwhile, grease a large baking sheet or line with parchment. Unroll pizza dough on baking sheet. Roll or pat dough to a 15 x 12-inch large rectangle. Top dough with beef filling, keeping within 1½ inches of edges. Fold edges over filling, pleating as needed.

③ Bake tart 15 minutes or until crust is golden. Top with blue cheese, and, if desired, oregano and pizza seasoning.

PER SERVING 525 cal, 23 g fat (10 g sat. fat), 74 mg chol, 1,041 mg sodium, 49 g carb, 2 g fiber, 31 g pro

Beefy Pasta Salad

Beefy Pasta Salad ♥

This salad is served slightly warm or at room temperature—perfect for experiencing the flavors of food most intensely.

MAKES 4 servings **START TO FINISH** 30 minutes

- 1 cup dried multigrain penne pasta (about 3½ ounces)
- 2 ears of corn, husks and silks removed

  Nonstick cooking spray
- 12 ounces boneless beef sirloin steak, cut into thin bite-size strips, or 2 cups shredded cooked beef pot roast (10 ounces)
- 1 cup cherry tomatoes, halved
- ¼ cup shredded fresh basil
- 2 tablespoons finely shredded Parmesan cheese
- 3 tablespoons white wine vinegar
- 2 tablespoons olive oil
- 1 clove garlic, minced
- ¼ teaspoon salt
- ⅛ teaspoon black pepper

  Finely shredded Parmesan cheese (optional)

① In a 4- to 6-quart Dutch oven cook pasta according to package directions, adding corn during the last 3 minutes of cooking time. Using tongs, transfer corn to a large cutting board. Drain pasta. Rinse in cold water and drain again; set aside. Cool corn until easy to handle.

② Meanwhile, coat an large unheated nonstick skillet with cooking spray. Preheat skillet over medium-high heat. Add beef strips. Cook for 4 to 6 minutes or until slightly pink in the center, stirring occasionally. (If using shredded beef, cook until heated through.) Remove from heat and cool slightly.

③ On a cutting board, place an ear of corn pointed end down. Holding corn firmly at stem end to keep in place, use a sharp knife to cut corn from cobs, leaving corn in planks. Rotate cob to cut corn from all sides. Repeat with the remaining ear of corn. In a large bowl combine pasta, beef, tomatoes, basil, and 2 tablespoons Parmesan cheese.

④ In a screw-top jar combine vinegar, oil, garlic, salt, and pepper. Cover and shake well. Pour over pasta mixture; toss gently to coat. Gently fold in corn planks or place corn planks on individual servings. Serve immediately. If desired, garnish with additional Parmesan cheese.

PER SERVING 322 cal, 12 g fat (3 g sat. fat), 38 mg chol, 256 mg sodium, 27 g carb, 4 g fiber, 26 g pro

Simple Beef and Noodles

Simple Beef and Noodles

Quick comfort food is not an oxymoron—and this dish proves the point deliciously.

MAKES 4 servings **PREP** 10 minutes **COOK** 20 minutes

- 1   17-ounce package refrigerated cooked beef tips with gravy
- ½   teaspoon dried basil, crushed
- ¼   teaspoon black pepper
- 1   10.75-ounce can condensed golden mushroom soup
- ½   cup beef broth
- 1½   cups sliced fresh mushrooms
- 1   cup packaged peeled baby carrots, halved lengthwise
- ⅓   cup thinly sliced onion (1 small)
- 1   12-ounce package frozen egg noodles

① In a large saucepan combine beef tips with gravy, basil, and pepper. Stir in soup and broth. Bring to boiling. Add mushrooms, carrots, and onion. Return to boiling; reduce heat to low. Simmer, covered, for 20 to 25 minutes or until vegetables are tender, stirring frequently.

② Meanwhile, cook noodles according to package directions; drain. Serve meat mixture over noodles.

PER SERVING 458 cal, 12 g fat (4 g sat. fat), 150 mg chol, 1,349 mg sodium, 61 g carb, 4 g fiber, 27 g pro

Chicken Fried Steak

Chicken Fried Steak ♥

This lightened-up version of the classic diner dish call for egg whites, fat-free milk, cornflakes, and minimal oil to achieve the same crispy results as the original recipe.

MAKES 4 servings **PREP** 20 minutes **COOK** 10 minutes

- 4   4- to 5-ounce boneless beef chuck top blade steaks or cubed steaks, cut ½ inch thick
- ⅓   cup all-purpose flour
- ½   teaspoon Montreal or Kansas City steak seasoning
- ¼   teaspoon salt
- ¼   cup refrigerated or frozen egg product, thawed
- 2   tablespoons fat-free milk
- 1   cup crushed cornflakes (2 cups whole flakes)
       Nonstick cooking spray
- 1   teaspoon butter
- ¼   cup finely chopped onion
- 1   clove garlic, minced
- ¾   cup fat-free milk
- 1   tablespoon all-purpose flour
- ¼   teaspoon Montreal or Kansas City steak seasoning

① Trim fat from steaks. If necessary, place each steak between two pieces of plastic wrap and pound lightly with the flat side of a meat mallet to ½-inch thickness.

② In a shallow dish combine the ⅓ cup flour, the ½ teaspoon steak seasoning, and salt. In another shallow dish, combine egg and the 2 tablespoons milk. Place crushed cornflakes in a third shallow dish. Dip steaks into flour mixture, turning to coat evenly. Dip into egg mixture, then into cornflakes, turning to coat evenly.

③ Coat a very large nonstick skillet with cooking spray; heat skillet over medium-high heat. Add steaks to skillet. Cook for 10 to 12 minutes for medium-rare (145°F) to medium (160°F), turning once halfway through cooking. Remove steaks from skillet; cover and keep warm.

④ For the gravy, in the same skillet heat butter over medium heat until melted. Add onion and garlic to skillet; cook for 3 to 5 minutes or until onion is tender. Stir to scrape up any crusty browned bits. In a small bowl whisk together milk, flour, and steak seasoning until smooth. Add all at once to onion mixture. Cook and stir until thickened and bubbly. Cook and stir for 1 minute more. Serve steaks with gravy. If desired, sprinkle with pepper.

PER SERVING 317 cal, 13 g fat (5 g sat. fat), 78 mg chol, 400 mg sodium, 22 g carb, 1 g fiber, 27 g pro

Peppered Steaks with Roasted Beets

Beets are sweet, earthy, and nutritious. They contain high levels of phytochemicals that promote heart health, and they're rich in vitamins and minerals as well.

MAKES 4 servings **START TO FINISH** 30 minutes

- 2 pounds small red and/or golden beets with tops
  Olive oil
  Salt and freshly ground black pepper
- 1 pound boneless beef sirloin steak, 1 inch thick
- 1 teaspoon cracked black pepper
  Nonstick cooking spray
- 1 tablespoon deli-style mustard
- 1 teaspoon packed brown sugar
- ½ ounce cream cheese, softened
- ½ teaspoon dried Italian seasoning

① Trim tops from beets, reserving tops. Peel beets and cut into wedges. Place in a 1½-quart microwave-safe casserole dish. Cover with vented clear plastic wrap. Cook on high for 9 to 12 minutes or until tender, stirring once. Meanwhile, rinse and drain reserved tops well. Tear 1 cup greens; set aside. Carefully uncover beets and drain. Toss with 1 tablespoon olive oil, ⅛ teaspoon salt, ⅛ teaspoon pepper, and the torn greens.

② Meanwhile, season both sides of steak with ¼ teaspoon salt and 1 teaspoon cracked black pepper. Lightly coat a grill pan or cast-iron skillet with cooking spray. Heat over medium-high heat. Add meat to pan. Cook 5 minutes per side or to desired doneness. Meanwhile, in a small saucepan combine 2 tablespoons water, mustard, and brown sugar. Cook over medium heat until just bubbly.

③ In a small bowl combine cream cheese and Italian seasoning. Cut steak into 4 serving-size pieces. Transfer to serving plates. Serve roasted beets alongside steaks and top with mustard sauce.

PER SERVING 418 cal, 27 g fat (11 g sat. fat), 83 mg chol, 418 mg sodium, 17 g carb, 4 g fiber, 27 g pro

Mexican Beef and Tortillas

This dish goes together in 20 minutes—less time than it would take to drive to the nearest fast-food Mexican restaurant—and it's a whole lot more healthful.

MAKES 4 servings **START TO FINISH** 20 minutes

- 8 corn tortillas
- 1 ounce refrigerated beef pot roast with juices
- 1 14½-ounce can diced tomatoes with green chiles
- 1 sweet green pepper, cut into strips
- 1 lime, cut into wedges
  Sour cream (optional)
  Fresh cilantro sprigs (optional)

① Wrap tortillas in microwave-safe paper towels. Heat on high 45 to 60 seconds or until warm. Cover; set aside.

② Microwave beef according to package directions. Meanwhile, place undrained tomatoes in small saucepan; heat through.

③ Remove meat, reserving juices. Cut in slices. Serve on warmed tortillas with tomatoes and green pepper strips. Pass lime wedges, and, if desired, sour cream and cilantro. Drizzle reserved juices.

PER SERVING 319 cal, 10 g fat (5 g sat. fat), 64 mg chol, 857 mg sodium, 34 g carb, 5 g fiber, 27 g pro

quick tip Use either white or yellow corn tortillas for this super-simple dish. The main difference between the two—other than the type of corn they're made from—is that yellow corn tortillas tend to be a bit thinner and more delicate than white tortillas.

Meatball Hoagies

Meatball Hoagies ♨

All this hearty sandwich needs to become a full meal are some crunchy veggies and dip on the side.

MAKES 6 servings **START TO FINISH** 30 minutes

1	medium onion, thinly sliced
1	medium red or green sweet pepper, seeded and cut into thin strips
1	tablespoon olive oil
1	16-ounce package frozen cooked Italian meatballs
2	cups refrigerated marinara sauce
¼	teaspoon crushed red pepper
6	slices provolone cheese (6 ounces)
6	hoagie buns or ciabatta rolls, split

① In a large saucepan cook onion and sweet pepper in hot oil over medium heat for 4 to 5 minutes or until crisp-tender. Add meatballs, marinara sauce, and crushed red pepper. Bring to boiling; reduce heat. Simmer, covered, about 15 minutes or until meatballs are heated through.

② To serve, place provolone cheese on bottom halves of rolls. Spoon meatball mixture onto each roll. If desired, broil sandwiches 4 to 5 inches from heat for 1 to 2 minutes or until cheese is melted.

PER SERVING 696 cal, 29 g fat (11 g sat. fat), 44 mg chol, 1,642 mg sodium, 84 g carb, 7 g fiber, 26 g pro

quick tip To lighten up this hearty sandwich a bit, substitute turkey meatballs for the beef meatballs.

Picante Pot Roast

Slices of ripe avocado contribute a creamy, buttery element to this homey pot roast dish.

MAKES 4 servings **START TO FINISH** 20 minutes

1	16- to 17-ounce package refrigerated cooked beef pot roast with juices
1½	cups sliced fresh mushrooms
1	cup bottled picante sauce
1	14-ounce can chicken broth
1	cup quick-cooking couscous
2	tablespoons snipped fresh cilantro
	Sour cream (optional)
	Chopped fresh tomato (optional)
	Sliced avocado (optional)

① Transfer liquid from pot roast package to a large skillet; add mushrooms and picante sauce. Cut pot roast into 1- to 1½-inch pieces; add to skillet. Bring to boiling; reduce heat. Simmer, covered, for 10 minutes.

② Meanwhile, in a medium saucepan bring broth to boiling. Stir in couscous; cover and remove from heat. Let stand about 5 minutes or until liquid is absorbed. Fluff couscous with a fork. Stir in cilantro.

③ Spoon pot roast over couscous. If desired, serve with sour cream, tomato, and/or avocado.

PER SERVING 370 cal, 9 g fat (3 g sat. fat), 61 mg chol, 1,268 mg sodium, 44 g carb, 3 g fiber, 31 g pro

Picante Pot Roast

Meatballs Stroganoff

Frozen meatballs are a great thing to have in the freezer. Switch up the sauces—try a creamy sauce like this one night and a tomatoey marinara the next—for two different meals.

MAKES 6 servings **START TO FINISH** 30 minutes

- 1 12- to 16-ounce package frozen cooked meatballs
- 1 cup lower-sodium beef broth
- 1 4-ounce can (drained weight) sliced mushrooms, drained
- 1 8-ounce carton sour cream
- 2 tablespoons all-purpose flour
- ½ cup milk
- 1 tablespoon Dijon mustard
- 4 cups hot cooked wide egg noodles
  Snipped fresh parsley (optional)

① In a large skillet combine meatballs, broth, and mushrooms. Bring to boiling; reduce heat. Cover; simmer about 15 minutes or until meatballs are heated through.

② In a small bowl stir together sour cream and flour. Whisk in milk and mustard. Stir sour cream mixture into skillet. Cook and stir until thickened and bubbly. Cook and stir for 1 minute more. Serve over hot cooked noodles. If desired, sprinkle with snipped fresh parsley.

PER SERVING 424 cal, 25 g fat (12 g sat. fat), 73 mg chol, 696 mg sodium, 36 g carb, 3 g fiber, 16 g pro

Meatballs Stroganoff

Sweet-and-Sour Meatballs

This bright and colorful sweet-and-sour dish served over noodles is a big hit with kids of all ages.

MAKES 4 servings **START TO FINISH** 30 minutes

- 1 20-ounce can pineapple chunks
- ¾ cup maple syrup or maple-flavor syrup
- ½ cup cider vinegar
- 1 12- to 16-ounce package frozen cooked meatballs
- 2 medium sweet red and/or green peppers
- ¼ cup cold water
- 2 tablespoons cornstarch
- ½ teaspoon salt
- 2 cups hot cooked Asian noodles or rice
  Sliced green onions (optional)

① Drain pineapple, reserving liquid. Set pineapple chunks aside. In a large saucepan stir together pineapple liquid, syrup, and vinegar. Add meatballs. Bring to boiling; reduce heat. Simmer, covered, for 15 minutes.

② Meanwhile, remove seeds from sweet peppers, then cut peppers into ¾-inch pieces. Add to meatballs. Simmer, covered, for 5 minutes more.

③ In a small bowl stir together the water, cornstarch, and salt until smooth. Stir into meatball mixture. Cook and stir for 1 to 2 minutes, or until thickened and bubbly. Stir in pineapple chunks; heat through. Serve over hot cooked noodles and, if desired, sprinkle with green onions.

PER SERVING 667 cal, 23 g fat (9 g sat. fat), 30 mg chol, 972 mg sodium, 107 g carb, 5 g fiber, 14 g pro

Ravioli Skillet Lasagna

Ravioli Skillet Lasagna

Traditional lasagna—with precooking pasta, layering ingredients, and long baking times—can be a monumental endeavor. This quick stovetop version takes only 25 minutes, start to finish.

MAKES 4 servings **START TO FINISH** 25 minutes

- 2 cups chunk-style spaghetti sauce
- ½ cup water
- 4 cups packaged fresh baby spinach
- 1 16-ounce package frozen meat or cheese-filled ravioli (4½ cups)
- 1 egg, lightly beaten
- ½ of a 15-ounce carton ricotta cheese
- ¼ cup grated Romano or Parmesan cheese
  Grated Romano or Parmesan cheese

① In a large skillet combine spaghetti sauce and the water. Bring to boiling. Stir in spinach until it is wilted. Stir in ravioli. Return to boiling; reduce heat. Cover and cook over medium heat about 5 minutes or until ravioli are nearly tender, stirring once to prevent sticking.

② In a medium bowl combine the egg, ricotta cheese, and ¼ cup Romano cheese. In large mounds, spoon ricotta mixture over ravioli. Cover and cook over medium-low heat about 10 minutes or until ricotta is set and pasta is just tender. Sprinkle each serving with additional grated Romano or Parmesan cheese.

PER SERVING 490 cal, 21 g fat (10 g sat. fat), 146 mg chol, 1061 mg sodium, 53 g carb, 7 g fiber, 23 g pro

quick tip Any kind of ravioli you like—including fancy types stuffed with chicken, mushrooms, or spinach—are great choices for this quick skillet lasagna.

Tamale Pies

In this version of a long-standing family favorite, every diner gets his or her personal pie! Corn muffin mix makes the quick crust.

MAKES 4 servings **START TO FINISH** 30 minutes
OVEN 425°F

- 1 pound ground beef
- 1 pound tomatoes, chopped
- ½ cup pitted olives, coarsely chopped
- ½ teaspoon salt and black pepper
- 1 8.5-ounce box corn muffin mix
- ½ cup shredded cheddar cheese (2 ounces)
  Pitted olives, coarsely chopped tomatoes, and cilantro leaves (optional)

① Preheat oven to 425°F. In a large skillet cook beef until browned. Drain off fat. Add chopped tomatoes, olives, ¼ cup water, salt, and pepper. Cook, stirring occasionally, until heated through.

② Prepare corn muffin mix according to package directions. Divide hot ground beef among four 12- to 16-ounce casserole dishes. Top with muffin mix; sprinkle with cheddar cheese.

③ Bake for 15 to 17 minutes or until topping is lightly golden and cooked through. Top with olives, tomatoes, and cilantro.

PER SERVING 609 cal, 31 g fat (11 g sat. fat), 147 mg chol, 1,052 mg sodium, 49 g carb, 2 g fiber, 32 g pro

Tamale Pies

Mediterranean Mostaccioli

Sicilians like the little bit of sweetness that raisins add to savory dishes. They're optional here—but worth a try!

MAKES 4 servings **START TO FINISH** 25 minutes

- 4 ounces dried mostaccioli or gemelli pasta
- 2 cups sliced zucchini
- 8 ounces ground beef
- ½ of a medium eggplant, peeled and cubed (about 2½ cups)
- 1 14½-ounce can diced tomatoes with basil, oregano, and garlic
- 2 tablespoons tomato paste
- ½ cup shredded carrot
- ¼ cup snipped fresh basil
- 2 tablespoons raisins (optional)
- ¼ teaspoon ground cinnamon
- 1 tablespoon balsamic vinegar (optional)
- ½ cup shredded mozzarella cheese (2 ounces)

① Cook pasta according to package directions, adding zucchini during the last 2 minutes of cooking. Drain; keep warm.

② Meanwhile, for sauce, in a large skillet cook beef and eggplant over medium heat until meat is brown; drain off fat. Stir in undrained tomatoes, tomato paste, carrot, basil, raisins (if desired), and cinnamon. Bring to boiling; reduce heat. Simmer, uncovered, about 2 minutes, or to desired consistency, stirring occasionally. Remove from heat. If desired, stir in vinegar.

③ Transfer pasta to a serving dish. Spoon sauce over pasta. Sprinkle with cheese.

PER SERVING 334 cal, 11 g fat (5 g sat. fat), 47 mg chol, 672 mg sodium, 38 g carb, 4 g fiber, 21 g pro

Garlic Pork

This simple stir-fry offers a delicious combination of tastes and textures—garlicky pork and chewy Asian noodles complemented by crunchy ribbons of broccoli and carrots—plus a fresh touch of sliced green onions.

MAKES 4 servings **START TO FINISH** 25 minutes

- 1 7.7-ounce package fresh stir-fry noodles or 8 ounces dried fine egg noodles
- 12 ounces ground pork or beef
- 2 teaspoons bottled minced garlic (4 cloves)
- 2 teaspoons peanut oil or cooking oil
- 1 teaspoon toasted sesame oil
- 2 cups packaged shredded broccoli (broccoli slaw mix)
- 1 medium carrot, cut into thin 2-inch strips
- 1 tablespoon grated fresh ginger
- ¼ teaspoon crushed red pepper
- ¼ cup chicken broth
- ¼ cup bottled hoisin sauce
  Sliced green onion (optional)

① Prepare fresh noodles according to package directions, reserving seasoning packet for another use. Or cook dried noodles according to package directions; drain.

② Meanwhile, heat a large skillet or wok over medium-high heat. Add ground meat and garlic; cook until meat is brown. Drain off fat. Remove meat from wok.

③ Add peanut oil and sesame oil to wok. Add shredded broccoli, carrot, ginger, and crushed red pepper; stir-fry for 2 minutes. Stir in broth and hoisin sauce. Cook and stir until bubbly.

④ Stir noodles into vegetables. Stir in cooked meat; heat through. If desired, sprinkle servings with green onion.

PER SERVING 500 cal, 23 g fat (7 g sat. fat), 61 mg chol, 457 mg sodium, 51 g carb, 2 g fiber, 23 g pro

Carmelized Pork with Melon

Caramelized Pork with Melon ♥

Use either boneless or bone-in chops in this dish. Generally, though, meat cooked on the bone stays juicier.

MAKES 4 servings **START TO FINISH** 25 minutes

1	small cantaloupe
¼	cup orange juice
3	tablespoons hoisin sauce
4	center-cut pork chops, cut ½ inch thick
	Salt
	Black pepper
1	tablespoon vegetable oil
6	tablespoons thinly sliced green onions (3)
	Shredded napa cabbage (optional)

① Remove rind and seeds from cantaloupe; chop melon. Place 2 cups of the chopped melon in a food processor or blender; add orange juice. Cover and process until smooth. Transfer ½ cup of the pureed melon to a small bowl; stir in hoisin sauce. Strain the remaining pureed melon, reserving juice and discarding solids.

② Lightly sprinkle chops with salt and pepper. Generously brush both sides of chops with the hoisin sauce mixture. In a large skillet heat oil over medium heat. Add chops; cook for 6 to 8 minutes or until well browned and chops are (160°F), turning once halfway through cooking.

③ Meanwhile, combine the remaining chopped melon, strained juice, and green onions. Remove chops from skillet; add remaining hoisin sauce mixture to skillet. Cook and stir until heated through. Spoon onto 4 dinner plates. Top each with a chop. Add melon mixture to skillet to warm slightly. Serve over chops. Serve with cabbage, if desired.

PER SERVING 327 cal, 10 g fat (2 g sat. fat), 117 mg chol, 452 mg sodium, 19 g carb, 2 g fiber, 39 g pro

Garlic Pork and Sweet Potato Hash

Have a bottle of hot sauce on the table when you serve this hash for those who like to spice things up. A little heat balances the sweetness of the potatoes.

MAKES 4 servings **START TO FINISH** 30 minutes

3	sweet potatoes or yams, scrubbed and chopped (4 cups)
1½	pounds pork tenderloin
2	tablespoons reduced-sodium soy sauce
	Black pepper
3	tablespoons cooking oil
8	cloves garlic, peeled and thinly sliced
2	green onions, sliced
2	tablespoons honey
2	tablespoons water

① Place sweet potatoes in a large microwave-safe bowl. Cover with vented plastic wrap and cook on high for 8 minutes or until tender, stirring once halfway through cooking.

② Meanwhile, cut pork into 1-inch thick pieces. Butterfly slices by cutting a horizontal slit about three-fourths the way through the slice; open and flatten slightly, using the palm of your hand. Brush each slice with some of the soy sauce and sprinkle lightly with pepper.

③ In a large skillet heat oil over medium-high heat. Add garlic, cook until garlic begins to crisp and turn golden. Remove with a slotted spoon; set aside. Add pork slices to the skillet and cook 2 to 3 minutes on each side or until some pink remains in the center. Remove to a platter; cover and keep warm.

④ Add potatoes to the skillet. Cook, stirring occasionally, until beginning to crisp and turn golden on the edges. Add green onions; cook 1 minute more. Divide potatoes among individual shallow bowls or plates. Top with pork and garlic.

⑤ Return skillet to heat. Add honey, the water, and remaining soy sauce. Whisk to combine and heat just until bubbly. Drizzle over pork.

PER SERVING 451 cal, 16 g fat (3 g sat. fat), 107 mg chol, 449 mg sodium, 39 g carb, 4 g fiber, 37 g pro

quick tip Let the garlic become golden, but do not let it brown. Burnt garlic tastes bitter.

Mustard-Glazed Pork Chops

If you don't have apricot preserves, peach preserves—even orange marmalade—make good substitutes.

MAKES 4 servings **START TO FINISH** 25 minutes

- 4 ½-inch thick bone-in pork chops
- 2 teaspoons olive oil
- 1 large onion, cut in thin wedges
- ½ cup apricot preserves
- 1 tablespoon Dijon or spicy mustard
- ¼ cup water
- 1 teaspoon paprika
- ½ teaspoon ground nutmeg
  Fresh sage leaves (optional)

① Season pork with salt and pepper. In a large skillet heat olive oil over medium-high heat. Add pork and onion to skillet. Cook 3 minutes; turn pork and onion. Cook 3 minutes more.

② Meanwhile, in a small microwave-safe bowl combine preserves, mustard, the water, paprika, and nutmeg. Heat in microwave for 1 to 2 minutes or until melted. Pour over pork in skillet. Reduce heat to medium. Cook, covered, 10 minutes or until chops are 145°F .

③ Divide pork and onion among serving plates; top with sage, if desired.

PER SERVING 503 cal, 32 g fat (11 g sat. fat), 89 mg chol, 313 mg sodium, 31 g carb, 1 g fiber, 20 g pro

Pork and Potato Skillet  ♥

Frozen hash brown potatoes and frozen peas and carrots make this dish a minimal prep proposition. The only ingredient to chop is one small onion.

MAKES 4 servings **PREP** 10 minutes **COOK** 20 minutes

- 4 4-cup boneless pork loin chops
- ¾ teaspoon seasoned salt
- 2 tablespoons cooking oil
- ⅓ cup chopped onion (1 small)
- 1 medium red sweet pepper, cut into ¾-inch pieces
- 3 cups frozen diced hash brown potatoes
- 2 cups frozen peas and carrots
- 1 teaspoon dried thyme, crushed

① Evenly sprinkle both sides of meat with ½ teaspoon of the seasoned salt. In a very large skillet heat 1 tablespoon of the oil over medium-high heat. Cook chops in hot oil for 3 minutes. Turn chops. Cook for 3 minutes more or until brown. Remove chops from skillet.

② Carefully add remaining 1 tablespoon oil to skillet. Add onion and sweet pepper; cook and stir for 1 minute. Add potatoes, peas and carrots, thyme, and remaining ¼ teaspoon seasoned salt; mix well. Cook for 6 minutes, stirring frequently.

③ Place chops on potato mixture in skillet; cover. Reduce heat to medium. Cook for 7 to 9 minutes more or chops are 145°F and potatoes are brown.

PER SERVING 406 cal, 15 g fat (3 g sat. fat), 72 mg chol, 422 mg sodium, 39 g carb, 5 g fiber, 29 g pro

> New guidelines for cooking pork chops to 145°F mean they'll be juicier and more flavorful.

Pork and Noodle Salad

To bring out the nutty flavor of sesame seeds, toast them for a few minutes in a small nonstick skillet over low heat. Watch carefully, they burn in a flash!

MAKES 4 servings **PREP** 20 minutes **CHILL** 2 hours

- 4 ounces dried Chinese egg noodles or fine noodles, broken in half
- 1 recipe Soy-Sesame Vinaigrette
- ¾ pound fresh asparagus, trimmed and cut into 2-inch-long pieces
- 8 ounces cooked lean pork, cut into thin strips
- 2 carrots, cut into thin strips
  Sesame seeds (optional)
  Sliced green onions (optional)

① Cook pasta according to package directions; drain. Prepare Soy-Sesame Vinaigrette.

② Cook asparagus in a covered saucepan in a small amount of lightly salted boiling water for 4 to 6 minutes or until crisp-tender. Drain well.

③ In a large bowl combine noodles, asparagus, pork, and carrot. Cover and refrigerate for 2 to 24 hours.

④ To serve, pour Soy-Sesame Vinaigrette over salad; toss gently to coat. If desired, sprinkle salad with sesame seeds and green onions.

Soy-Sesame Vinaigrette In a screw-top jar combine ¼ cup reduced-sodium soy sauce, 2 tablespoons rice vinegar, 1 tablespoon salad oil, 1 tablespoon honey, and 1 teaspoon sesame oil. Cover and shake well to mix. Chill for 2 to 24 hours.

PER SERVING 328 cal, 12 g fat (3 g sat. fat), 76 mg chol, 974 mg sodium, 31 g carb, 2 g fiber, 24 g pro

Fettuccine alla Carbonara

This version of the classic Italian pasta dish goes together in 30 minutes. With a sauce of both bacon and prosciutto, butter, cream, white wine, and Parmesan cheese, it's a company-worthy dish.

MAKES 6 servings **START TO FINISH** 30 minutes

- 16 ounces packaged dried fettuccine
- 8 slices bacon
- 4 ounces sliced prosciutto
- 2 tablespoons finely chopped onion
- ¾ cup unsalted butter
- ⅓ cup dry white wine
- ½ cup whipping cream
- ½ cup milk
- ½ cup grated Parmesan cheese
- 1 tablespoon snipped fresh parsley
  Black pepper

① In a large pot cook pasta according to package directions; drain. Return pasta to pan; keep warm.

② Meanwhile, for sauce, in a large skillet cook bacon over medium heat until crisp. Drain well on paper towels; coarsely crumble. Chop prosciutto into ½-inch pieces; set aside.

③ In a medium saucepan cook onion in hot butter over medium heat for 4 minutes or until tender. Add prosciutto. Cook and stir over medium heat for 3 minutes. Remove pan from heat. Carefully add wine. Return to heat and bring to boiling. Boil gently, uncovered, for 5 minutes. Stir in the bacon, cream, and milk; bring to boiling. Boil gently, uncovered, for 5 minutes. Stir in ¼ cup of the Parmesan cheese and the parsley. Immediately pour sauce over pasta; stir gently to coat.

④ Divide pasta among 6 serving plates. Sprinkle each serving with remaining cheese. Season to taste with pepper. Serve immediately.

PER SERVING 722 cal, 43 g fat (22 g sat. fat), 108 mg chol, 705 mg sodium, 59 g carb, 3 g fiber, 22 g pro

Ham and Slaw Stuffed Peppers

Creamy and crunchy broccoli slaw is stuffed into sweet peppers in this dish—a hybrid of traditional stuffed peppers and stuffed tomatoes, which are served cold and stuffed with tuna or chicken salad.

MAKES 4 servings **START TO FINISH** 20 minutes

- 3 cups packaged shredded broccoli (broccoli slaw mix)
- 1 cup cubed cooked ham (about 6 ounces)
- ¼ cup bottled Parmesan ranch or peppercorn ranch salad dressing
- 4 small yellow, orange, red, and/or green sweet peppers
- 2 tablespoons sunflower kernels

① In a Dutch oven bring water to boiling. Meanwhile, for salad, in a large bowl combine shredded broccoli, ham, and salad dressing; set aside.

② Meanwhile, cut tops off peppers; remove and discard seeds and membranes. Place the pepper bottoms and tops in the boiling water. Reduce heat; cover and simmer for 3 minutes. Drain. Rinse with cold running water until cooled; drain again.

③ Place pepper halves, cut sides up, on plates. Mound salad into pepper halves, allowing any extra to overflow onto plates. Sprinkle with sunflower kernels. Replace pepper tops, if desired.

PER SERVING 190 cal, 13 g fat (3 g sat. fat), 24 mg chol, 597 mg sodium, 13 g carb, 4 g fiber, 9 g pro

quick tip This super-quick dish can be made 8 to 10 hours ahead of serving. Simply prepare the sweet peppers and filling, then store them separately, covered, in the refrigerator. Scoop the filling into the peppers right before serving.

Ham and Swiss Skillet

This cheesy egg dish makes a delicious brunch dish as well as a quick supper. Serve it with fresh fruit in the morning and a crisp green salad at night.

MAKES 4 servings **START TO FINISH** 30 minutes

- 1 tablespoon butter or margarine
- 1 cup sliced fresh mushrooms
- 2 tablespoons sliced green onion (1)
- ¾ cup finely chopped zucchini
- ¾ cup finely chopped cooked ham
- 6 eggs
- ¼ teaspoon dried thyme, crushed
- ¼ teaspoon caraway seeds
  Dash salt
  Dash black pepper
- ½ cup shredded Swiss cheese (2 ounces)

① Preheat broiler. In a large nonstick or well-seasoned broilerproof skillet heat butter on medium-high heat until melted. Add mushrooms and green onion; cook about 5 minutes or until tender, stirring occasionally. Stir in zucchini. Cook, covered, on medium-low heat for 2 to 3 minutes or until crisp-tender, stirring occasionally. Stir in ham.

② In a medium bowl beat eggs until blended but not foamy. Stir in thyme, caraway seeds, salt, and pepper. Pour eggs over vegetables in skillet.

③ Cook over medium heat. As mixture sets, run a spatula around edge of skillet, lifting egg mixture so uncooked portion flows underneath. Continue cooking and lifting edge until eggs are almost set (surface will be moist). Sprinkle with cheese.

④ Broil 4 to 5 inches from the heat for 1 to 2 minutes or just until top is set and cheese is melted. Cut into wedges.

PER SERVING 241 cal, 16 g fat (7 g sat. fat), 355 mg chol, 547 mg sodium, 3 g carb, 1 g fiber, 21 g pro

Ham and Swiss Skillet

Hawaiian Tacos

Mexican Chef's Salad

This recipe is a tasty way to use leftover cooked pork chops, steaks, or chicken breasts.

MAKES 4 servings **START TO FINISH** 30 minutes

4	cups torn iceberg or leaf lettuce
4	cups torn romaine or fresh spinach
4	ounces cooked pork, beef, or chicken, cut into bite-size strips (about 1 cup)
4	ounces Cheddar or Monterey Jack cheese, cut into bite-size strips (1 cup)
1	4- to 4.5-ounce can diced green chili peppers
¼	cup sliced ripe olives
2	medium tomatoes, cut into wedges, or 8 cherry tomatoes, halved
1	small green or red sweet pepper, cut into bite-size strips (½ cup)
1	cup corn chips
½	cup Thousand Island Dressing
¼	cup bottled salsa

① In a large bowl toss together greens. Divide among 4 large salad plates. Arrange meat, cheese, green chili peppers, olives, tomatoes, and sweet pepper strips on the greens. Sprinkle with corn chips.

② In a small bowl stir together the Thousand Island Dressing and the salsa. Drizzle over each salad.

PER SERVING 358 cal, 23 g fat (9 g sat. fat), 59 mg chol, 686 mg sodium, 20 g carb, 4 g fiber, 19 g pro

Mexican Chef's Salad

Hawaiian Tacos

If your taste leans toward milder flavors, substitute sweet or mild Italian sausage for the hot sausage.

MAKES 4 servings **START TO FINISH** 30 minutes

1	pound bulk hot Italian sausage
½	cup chopped onion
2	cloves garlic, minced
	Dash bottled hot pepper sauce
12	taco shells
1	recipe Hawaiian Pineapple Salsa
1	cup shredded cheddar cheese (4 ounces)

① In a large skillet cook sausage, onion, and garlic until sausage is browned and onion is tender; stir to break up sausage. Drain off fat. Stir in pepper sauce. Spoon meat into taco shells. Top with Hawaiian Pineapple Salsa and sprinkle with cheese.

Hawaiian Pineapple Salsa Combine 3 roma tomatoes, seeded and chopped; 1 cup seeded, chopped cucumber; 1 8-ounce can pineapple tidbits; ⅓ cup chopped onion; 1 to 2 fresh jalapeños, seeded and chopped (see note, below); 2 tablespoons snipped fresh cilantro; and 1 tablespoon brown sugar. Cover and refrigerate up to 2 hours. If refrigerated more than 30 minutes, serve salsa with slotted spoon.

PER SERVING 259 cal, 18 g fat (7 g sat. fat), 39 mg chol, 387 mg sodium, 16 g carb, 2 g fiber, 9 g pro

Note: Because chile peppers contain oils that can burn skin and eyes, avoid direct contact with them as much as possible. Wear plastic or rubber gloves when handling them. If hands touch the peppers, wash well with soap and warm water.

Ham and Cantaloupe Salad

The sweetness of the cantaloupe and saltiness of the ham is a tasty combination for a cool summer salad.

MAKES 4 servings   **PREP** 25 minutes

- ¼ cup unsweetened pineapple juice
- 1 tablespoon white wine vinegar
- 1 tablespoon salad oil
- 1½ teaspoons snipped fresh mint or ½ teaspoon dried mint, crushed
- 1 small cantaloupe, halved and seeded
- 8 ounces lean cooked ham, cut into bite-size strips (1½ cups)
- 2 green onions, thinly sliced
- 4 cups torn romaine lettuce
- 1 cup torn spinach
- ¼ cup sliced almonds, toasted (see quick tip, page 76)

① For the dressing, in a screw-top jar combine pineapple juice, white wine vinegar, salad oil, and mint. Cover and shake well.

② Coarsely chop half the melon; slice remaining melon. To serve, arrange melon slices on 4 plates. Add chopped melon, ham, green onions, and greens. Pour dressing over salad; toss lightly to coat. Sprinkle with almonds.

PER SERVING 217 cal, 11 g fat (2 g sat. fat), 31 mg chol, 776 mg sodium, 13 g carb, 3 g fiber, 18 g pro

Ham and Cantaloupe Salad

Incredible Quesadillas

If you like, use brown-and-serve turkey sausage links in these tropical-inspired quesadillas.

MAKES 4 servings   **START TO FINISH** 30 minutes
OVEN 300°F

- 1 recipe Pineapple Salsa
- 4 light brown-and-serve sausage links
- ½ cup shredded reduced-fat Mexican blend cheese
- 4 whole wheat flour tortillas
- 1 red onion, thinly sliced and separated into rings
- 2 tablespoons snipped fresh cilantro
  Fresh cilantro sprigs (optional)

① Preheat oven to 300°F. Prepare Pineapple Salsa; set aside. Cook sausage according to package directions; drain. Coarsely chop sausage; set aside.

② Divide cheese among tortillas, sprinkling on half of each tortilla. Top with sausage, 2 tablespoons of the Pineapple Salsa, some of the onion, and the snipped cilantro. Fold tortillas in half, pressing gently.

③ Preheat a medium nonstick skillet or griddle over medium heat. Two at a time, cook quesadillas in hot skillet for 2 to 3 minutes or until golden brown on bottoms. Turn quesadillas; cook for 2 to 3 minutes more or until golden brown on bottoms. Remove quesadillas from skillet to a baking sheet; keep warm in oven while cooking remaining quesadillas.

④ Garnish quesadillas with remaining onion slices and, if desired, cilantro sprigs. Serve quesadillas with Pineapple Salsa.

Pineapple Salsa: In a small bowl stir together ½ cup chopped fresh pineapple; ¼ cup chopped red sweet pepper; 2 tablespoons chopped red onion; 1 tablespoon snipped fresh cilantro; ½ a fresh serrano or jalapeño pepper, seeded and finely chopped (see note, page 47), ½ teaspoon finely shredded lime peel; and ⅛ teaspoon salt. Serve immediately or refrigerate in an airtight container up to 24 hours. Makes 1 cup.

PER SERVING 225 cal, 9 g fat (4 g sat. fat), 16 mg chol, 631 mg sodium, 19 g carb, 11 g fiber, 15 g pro

Incredible Quesadillas

Busy cooks rely on chicken (and turkey) because it is quick-cooking, inexpensive, and incredibly versatile. Team it with other fast-cooking ingredients and chicken is a sure winner at any table.

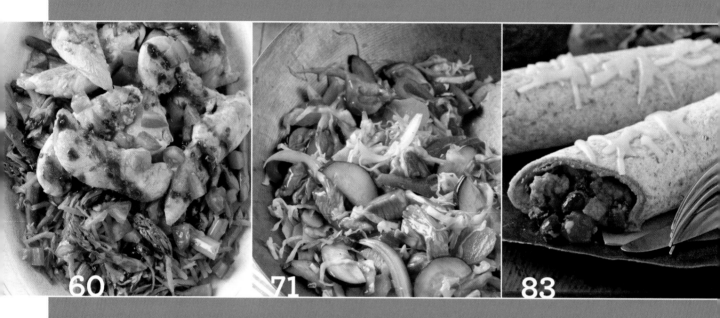

60   **71**   **83**

QUICK POULTRY

Pesto Chicken with Summer Squash ♥

Pesto is sold in jars on the grocery-store shelf as well as in small tubs in the refrigerated section. If you have a choice, go with refrigerated pesto—it tastes fresher and has better color.

MAKES 4 servings   **PREP** 5 minutes   **BROIL** 10 minutes

- 1 pound skinless, boneless chicken breast halves
- 2 zucchini, halved lengthwise
- 2 yellow summer squash, halved lengthwise
- ¼ teaspoon salt
- ¼ teaspoon black pepper
- ¼ cup purchased basil pesto

① Preheat broiler. Sprinkle chicken, zucchini, and yellow squash with salt and black pepper. Place chicken breast halves on the unheated rack of a broiler pan. Broil about 5 inches from the heat for 5 minutes.

② Turn chicken; place vegetables on rack with chicken. Spoon pesto over chicken and vegetables. Broil for 5 to 7 minutes more or until chicken is no longer pink (170°F) and vegetables are tender.

③ Slice chicken and serve with zucchini and yellow squash pieces.

PER SERVING 230 cal, 9 g fat (2 g sat. fat), 71 mg chol, 364 mg sodium, 8 g carb, 3 g fiber, 30 g pro

Pesto Chicken with Summer Squash

Chicken and Pepper Saute ♥

Any dry white white—Pinot Grigio, Chardonnay, Sauvignon Blanc, or simply white table wine—works well in this simple saute.

MAKES 4 servings   **PREP** 15 minutes   **COOK** 14 minutes

- ¼ cup all-purpose flour
- ¼ teaspoon salt
- ¼ teaspoon black pepper
- 4 small skinless, boneless chicken breast halves (1 to 1¼ pounds total)
- 1 tablespoon canola oil or olive oil
- 2 small red and/or green sweet peppers, seeded and cut into bite-size strips
- 1 small onion, halved and sliced
- 2 cloves garlic, minced
- 3 plum tomatoes, seeded and chopped (1 cup)
- ⅔ cup dry white wine or reduced-sodium chicken broth
- 1 tablespoon lemon juice
- 2 tablespoons snipped fresh parsley

① In a shallow dish combine flour, salt, and black pepper. Dip chicken breast halves in flour mixture, turning to coat both sides.

② In a large skillet heat oil over medium heat. Add chicken to skillet. Cook for 8 to 12 minutes or until chicken is no longer pink (170°F), turning once. Remove chicken from skillet and cut up, if desired; cover to keep warm.

③ Add sweet peppers, onion, and garlic to skillet. Cook and stir for 2 minutes. Remove skillet from heat. Add tomatoes, wine, and lemon juice to skillet. Return to heat. Bring to boiling; reduce heat. Boil gently about 4 minutes or until liquid is slightly thickened. Stir in parsley.

④ Serve pepper mixture and chicken in shallow bowls.

PER SERVING 236 cal, 5 g fat (1 g sat. fat), 66 mg chol, 138 mg sodium, 12 g carb, 2 g fiber, 28 g pro

Chicken and Pepper Sauté

Pan-Roasted Chicken with Shallots

Pan-Roasted Chicken with Shallots ♨ ♥

If you like, serve this chicken-and-veggie dish with hot cooked rice or couscous.

MAKES 4 servings **START TO FINISH** 20 minutes

- 8 shallots or 1 large onion
- 4 medium skinless, boneless chicken breast halves (1 to 1¼ pounds total)
  Salt and black pepper
- 1 tablespoon olive oil
- 1 medium zucchini, halved lengthwise and sliced ¼ inch thick
- ¼ cup snipped fresh parsley

① Peel shallots; halve small shallots and quarter large shallots. If using onion, cut into thin wedges (1 cup shallots or onion wedges); set aside. Sprinkle chicken lightly with salt and pepper. In a large skillet heat oil over medium-high heat. Reduce heat to medium. Add chicken; cook for 2 minutes.

② Turn chicken. Add shallots to skillet. Sprinkle shallots lightly with additional salt and pepper. Cook for 8 to 10 minutes more or until chicken is no longer pink (170°F), stirring shallots frequently and turning chicken, if necessary, to brown evenly. If necessary, add additional oil to prevent sticking. Reduce heat to medium-low if chicken or shallots brown too quickly.

③ Transfer chicken and shallots to a serving platter. Cover to keep warm. Add zucchini to skillet. Cook and stir for 3 to 5 minutes or until crisp-tender. Serve zucchini with chicken. Sprinkle with parsley.

PER SERVING 193 cal, 5 g fat (1 g sat. fat), 66 mg chol, 231 mg sodium, 9 g carb, 1 g fiber, 28 g pro

Sauteed Chicken Breasts with Simple Chive Sauce ♥

The little bit of flour left in the pan from sautéing the chicken breasts helps to thicken the wine sauce just enough to give it body.

MAKES 4 servings **START TO FINISH** 30 minutes

- 4 4-ounce skinless, boneless chicken breast halves
- ¼ teaspoon salt
- ¼ teaspoon black pepper
- 3 tablespoons whole wheat flour
- 1 tablespoon olive oil
- ½ cup finely chopped shallots
- ½ cup dry white wine or reduced-sodium chicken broth
- 1 cup reduced-sodium chicken broth or chicken stock
- 1 tablespoon snipped fresh chives

① Sprinkle chicken breasts with salt and pepper. Place flour in a shallow dish; dip chicken in flour, turning to coat all sides.

② Preheat a large skillet over medium-high heat. Add oil to skillet; swirl to lightly coat skillet. Add chicken breasts, smooth sides down; cook about 5 minutes or until the chicken is golden brown.

③ Turn chicken; cook for 4 to 5 minutes more or until chicken is no longer pink (170°F). Transfer chicken to a warm serving platter; set aside.

④ For the sauce, cook the shallots in the hot skillet for 2 minutes, stirring frequently. Carefully add wine; cook about 1 minute or until liquid is reduced by half, stirring to scrape up any browned bits from skillet.

⑤ Add chicken broth to skillet; cook for 3 to 4 minutes or until liquid is reduced by half. Stir in chives. Return chicken to skillet; heat through. Serve immediately.

PER SERVING 217 cal, 5 g fat (1 g sat. fat), 66 mg chol, 366 mg sodium, 9 g carb, 1 g fiber, 28 g pro

Pesto Chicken, Spinach, Squash, and Tomatoes over Pasta 🍲 ♥

This veggie-packed chicken and pasta dish needs only something to sip to make a complete meal.

MAKES 4 servings **START TO FINISH** 25 minutes

- 1 tablespoon extra virgin olive oil
- 1 pound skinless, boneless chicken breast halves, cut into thin bite-size strips
- 2 cups chopped yellow summer squash and/or zucchini
- 2 tablespoons refrigerated basil pesto
- 3 cups fresh spinach
- 1 cup cherry tomatoes, halved
  Kosher salt
  Freshly ground black pepper
- 2 cups hot cooked whole grain or whole wheat pasta
- 2 tablespoons finely shredded Asiago or Parmesan cheese

① In a large skillet heat olive oil over medium-high heat. Add chicken strips and squash; cook and stir for 4 to 6 minutes or until chicken is no longer pink. Stir in pesto. Add spinach and tomatoes; cook and toss about 1 minute or just until spinach is wilted. Season to taste with kosher salt and pepper. Serve over hot cooked pasta and sprinkle with cheese.

PER SERVING 347 cal, 12 g fat (2 g sat. fat), 71 mg chol, 310 mg sodium, 25 g carb, 4 g fiber, 35 g pro

Triple-Mango Chicken ♥

If you don't have a ripe mango on hand, the fresh mango in jars in the refrigerated section of the produce aisle are perfectly fine to use in this recipe.

MAKES 4 servings **START TO FINISH** 20 minutes

- 1 tablespoon olive oil
- 4 skinless, boneless chicken breast halves
- 1 mango, seeded, peeled, and cubed
- ½ cup mango-blend fruit drink
- ¼ cup mango chutney
- 2 zucchini, thinly sliced lengthwise
  Salt
  Crushed red pepper

① In very large skillet heat oil over medium-high heat; reduce to medium. Add chicken; cook for 6 minutes; turn chicken. Add mango cubes, mango drink, and chutney. Cook for 4 to 6 minutes or until chicken is no longer pink, stirring occasionally.

② Meanwhile, place zucchini and ¼ cup water in a microwave-safe two-quart square dish. Cover with vented plastic wrap. Cook on high for 2 to 3 minutes, stirring once; drain. Serve chicken with zucchini. Season with salt and crushed red pepper.

PER SERVING 274 cal, 9 g fat (1 g sat. fat), 66 mg chol, 277 mg sodium, 22 g carb, 2 g fiber, 28 g pro

quick tip Mango nectar, carrot juice, or orange juice may be substituted for the mango-blend drink.

Balsamic Chicken
and Vegetables

Chicken Piccata

Chicken Piccata 🍲 ♥

This classic Italian dish has a wonderful combination of complementary flavors. Garlic, the brightness of the lemon, and the vinegary piquance of the capers is softened by just a bit of butter.

MAKES 4 servings **START TO FINISH** 25 minutes

- 2 8-ounce skinless, boneless chicken breasts, cut in half horizontally
- ¼ teaspoon salt
- ¼ teaspoon black pepper
- 1 tablespoon butter
- 2 cloves garlic, minced
- ½ cup reduced-sodium chicken broth
- 1 medium lemon, thinly sliced
- 2 tablespoons capers
- 1 tablespoon snipped fresh parsley

① Place each chicken breast portion between two pieces of plastic wrap. Using the flat side of a meat mallet, pound chicken lightly until about ¼ inch thick. Remove plastic wrap. Sprinkle chicken with salt and pepper.

② In a large skillet melt butter over medium-high heat. Add chicken; cook for 6 to 8 minutes or until browned and no longer pink in center, turning once halfway through cooking. Remove chicken from skillet; set aside.

③ Add garlic to the hot skillet; cook for 30 seconds to 1 minute or until lightly browned. Add chicken broth to skillet, scraping up any browned bits from the skillet. Bring to boiling. Add lemon slices and capers. Cover; reduce heat to low. Cook for 4 to 5 minutes or until lemon slices are softened and releasing juices. Return chicken to skillet; heat through.

④ To serve, spoon sauce over chicken. Sprinkle with fresh parsley.

PER SERVING 161 cal, 4 g fat (2 g sat. fat), 73 mg chol, 440 mg sodium, 4 g carb, 2 g fiber, 27 g pro

Sautéed Chicken with Pasta

Just a smidgen of Dijon mustard infuses the pan sauce with flavor in this simple pasta dish.

MAKES 4 servings **START TO FINISH** 30 minutes

- 8 ounces angel hair pasta
- ½ teaspoon dried thyme, crushed
- ½ teaspoon salt
- ¼ teaspoon black pepper
- 2 skinless, boneless chicken breast halves, halved horizontally (about 12 ounces total)
- 2 tablespoons olive oil
- 8 ounces sliced mushrooms (3 cups)
- 1 small red onion, halved and sliced (about 1 cup)
- 1½ teaspoons bottled minced garlic
- 1½ cups reduced-sodium chicken broth
- 1 tablespoon all-purpose flour
- 1 teaspoon Dijon mustard
- 4 plum tomatoes, cut into thin wedges
- ¼ cup chopped fresh parsley

① Cook pasta according to package directions; drain.

② Meanwhile, combine dried thyme, ¼ teaspoon of the salt and pepper in a small bowl. Sprinkle on both sides of each chicken breast piece. Heat 1 tablespoon of the oil in an extra large skillet over medium-high heat. Add chicken to skillet. Reduce heat to medium and cook until golden and cooked through (170°F), about 6 minutes, turning once. Remove chicken from skillet; cover and keep warm.

③ Add remaining oil to the skillet. Heat over medium-high heat. Stir in mushrooms, onion, and garlic. Cook, stirring occasionally, until onion is tender, about 5 minutes. Whisk together broth, flour, mustard, and remaining salt; add to skillet. Cook and stir until slightly thickened and bubbly. Stir in tomatoes and parsley; heat through.

④ Serve chicken and mushroom sauce with pasta.

PER SERVING 426 cal, 9 g fat (2 g sat. fat), 49 mg chol, 604 mg sodium, 53 g carb, 4 g fiber, 31 g pro

Chicken Marinara with Mushrooms

The base for this sauce is a jar of spaghetti sauce that gets a flavor boost from garlic, herbs, and dry white wine.

MAKES 6 servings **START TO FINISH** 20 minutes

- 12 ounces dried linguine or spaghetti
- 4 cloves garlic, minced
- 2 tablespoons margarine or butter
- 1 pound skinless, boneless chicken breast halves, cut into thin bite-size strips
- ½ teaspoon dried parsley, crushed
- ½ teaspoon dried basil, crushed
- ¼ teaspoon dried thyme, crushed
- 6 ounces fresh mushrooms, sliced
- 1 27.5-ounce jar spaghetti sauce
- ½ cup dry white wine
- 2 teaspoons sugar (optional)

① Cook pasta according to package directions; drain and keep warm. Meanwhile, in a large skillet cook garlic in hot margarine for 30 seconds. Add half the chicken and half of each the herb. Cook and stir for 3 to 4 minutes or until chicken is no longer pink. Remove chicken, reserving drippings in skillet. Cook remaining chicken and herbs.

② Add mushrooms to drippings in skillet. Cook and stir about 3 minutes or until tender. Add spaghetti sauce, wine, and, if desired, sugar. Return chicken to skillet; heat through. Serve over hot pasta.

PER SERVING 426 cal, 7 g fat (1 g sat. fat), 40 mg chol, 128 mg sodium, 64 g carb, 4 g fiber, 25 g pro

Honey-and-Ginger-Crusted Chicken ♥

If you like some heat in your food, add a little more than a dash of cayenne pepper to the spice mix for the chicken.

MAKES 4 servings **PREP** 10 minutes **BAKE** 20 minutes
OVEN 350°F

   Nonstick cooking spray
- 4 skinless, boneless chicken breast halves (about 1¼ pounds total)
- 1 tablespoon honey
- 2 teaspoons orange juice
- ¼ teaspoon salt
- ¼ teaspoon ground ginger
- ¼ teaspoon black pepper
   Dash cayenne pepper (optional)
- ¾ cup cornflakes, crushed
- ½ teaspoon dried parsley flakes or 1 tablespoon snipped fresh parsley

① Preheat oven to 350°F. Line a shallow baking pan with foil; coat foil with cooking spray. Place chicken in prepared pan. In a small bowl combine honey, orange juice, salt, ginger, black pepper, and, if desired, cayenne pepper. Brush honey mixture over chicken. In another small bowl combine cornflakes and dried parsley flakes (if using). Sprinkle cornflake mixture or plain cornflakes over chicken.

② Bake, uncovered, for 20 to 25 minutes or until chicken is tender and no longer pink (170°F). Sprinkle chicken with fresh parsley (if using) before serving.

PER SERVING 198 cal, 2 g fat (1 g sat. fat), 82 mg chol, 257 mg sodium, 9 g carb, 0 g fiber, 33 g pro

> Mild flavor, quick to fix, and supremely versatile, chicken might well be America's favorite bird.

Chicken and Vegetable Spaghetti

Chicken and Vegetable Spaghetti ☕ ♥

Broccolini is a cross between broccoli and a variety of Chinese broccoli with smaller florets and longer, thinner stalks. It has a sweet flavor, with hints of broccoli and asparagus.

MAKES 4 servings **START TO FINISH** 35 minutes

2	cups frozen, peeled pearl onions
12	ounces dried spaghetti
8	ounces skinless, boneless chicken breast halves, cut into bite-size pieces
1	tablespoon olive oil
8	ounces broccolini, trimmed, or broccoli, cut in pieces
1	teaspoon dried parsley flakes (optional)
½	teaspoon salt (optional)
	Crushed red pepper (optional)
8	ounces container yellow or red cherry tomatoes (1¼ cups)
1	cup chicken broth

① In large pot of water cook onions for 3 minutes. Remove with slotted spoon; set aside. In same water cook pasta according to package directions. Reserve 1 cup cooking water. Drain pasta; set aside.

② Meanwhile, in a large skillet cook chicken in hot oil over medium-high heat for 3 to 4 minutes, stirring occasionally. Add broccolini and onions. If desired, sprinkle parsley, salt, and red pepper. Cook, stirring frequently, for 5 minutes. Add tomatoes, broth, the reserved cooking water, and spaghetti. Simmer, covered, about 5 minutes or until broth is slightly reduced and vegetables are tender.

PER SERVING 453 cal, 6 g fat (1 g sat. fat), 34 mg chol, 318 mg sodium, 71 g carb, 5 g fiber, 27 g pro

quick tip This recipe calls for reserved pasta-cooking water to make the sauce. It's always a good idea to scoop out a cup or so of the pasta-cooking water before draining it in case it's needed to thin a stiff sauce. Water that has had pasta cooked in it contains starch, which gives body to the sauce which helps it cling to the pasta.

Chicken and Rice Scramble

This quick supper dish is essentially a frittata, open-face Italian omelet. If you happen to have any leftover roasted or steamed vegetables, toss those in with the chicken and rice.

MAKES 4 servings **START TO FINISH** 20 minutes

1	8.8-ounce pouch cooked Spanish-style rice
2	tablespoons olive oil
1	medium zucchini or yellow summer squash, halved lengthwise and sliced
2	cups cubed cooked chicken
8	eggs, lightly beaten
½	cup milk
¼	teaspoon salt
¼	teaspoon black pepper
½	cup finely shredded Mexican cheese blend (2 ounces)

① Preheat broiler. Microwave rice according to package directions. Meanwhile, in a large broilerproof skillet heat oil over medium heat; add zucchini. Cook and stir for 2 minutes; stir in chicken and rice.

② In a large bowl combine eggs, milk, salt, and pepper; pour over chicken mixture in skillet. Cook, without stirring, until mixture begins to set on the bottom and around the edges. Using a large spatula, lift and fold partially cooked eggs so the uncooked portion flows underneath. Continue cooking over medium heat for 2 to 3 minutes or until egg mixture is cooked through but still glossy and moist. Remove from heat. Sprinkle with cheese.

③ Broil 4 to 5 inches from heat for 1 to 2 minutes or until cheese is melted.

PER SERVING 512 cal, 28 g fat (9 g sat. fat), 500 mg chol, 667 mg sodium, 22 g carb, 1 g fiber, 39 g pro

Curried Chicken with Cabbage, Apple, and Onion ♥

To save time and mess, use shredded cabbage from the salad section of the produce aisle.

MAKES 4 servings **PREP** 15 minutes **COOK** 11 minutes

- 1 teaspoon curry powder
- ¼ teaspoon salt
- ¼ teaspoon black pepper
- 4 small skinless, boneless chicken breast halves (1 to 1¼ pounds total)
- 2 teaspoons olive oil
- 2 teaspoons butter
- 1 medium onion, sliced and separated into rings
- 3 cups shredded cabbage
- 2 red-skin cooking apples (such as Rome or Jonathan), cored and thinly sliced
- ½ cup apple juice

① In a small bowl combine ½ teaspoon of the curry powder, the salt, and pepper. Sprinkle spice mixture evenly over chicken; rub in with your fingers.

② In a large nonstick skillet heat oil over medium-high heat. Add chicken. Cook for 8 to 12 minutes or until no longer pink (170°F), turning once. Transfer chicken to a platter. Cover to keep warm.

③ Melt butter in the hot skillet. Add onion. Cook about 5 minutes or until tender, stirring occasionally. Stir in cabbage, apples, and apple juice. Sprinkle with the remaining ½ teaspoon curry powder. Cook for 3 to 4 minutes or just until apples and vegetables are tender, stirring occasionally.

④ To serve, divide chicken and cabbage mixture among 4 dinner plates.

PER SERVING 237 cal, 6 g fat (2 g sat. fat), 71 mg chol, 231 mg sodium, 19 g carb, 4 g fiber, 27 g pro

Snappy Chicken Stir-Fry

If you'd like, use 6 ounces of fresh snow pea pods—strings removed—in place of the frozen peas. Fresh peas will be crisper than frozen peas.

MAKES 4 servings **START TO FINISH** 20 minutes

- 1 6-ounce package frozen pea pods
- 1 pound boneless, skinless chicken breasts
- ¼ cup orange juice
- 2 tablespoons water
- 2 tablespoons soy sauce
- 2 teaspoons cornstarch
- 1 tablespoon cooking oil
   Hot cooked rice
   Chopped peanuts (optional)

① Let pea pods stand at room temperature to partially thaw. Meanwhile, cut chicken into 1-inch pieces. In a small bowl stir together orange juice, the water, soy sauce, and cornstarch.

② Preheat a wok or large skillet over high heat. Add cooking oil. Stir-fry chicken, half at a time, for 2 to 3 minutes or until no pink remains. Add more oil as necessary. Return all chicken to wok. Push chicken to the sides of the wok. Stir orange juice mixture and add to center of wok. Cook and stir until thickened and bubbly.

③ Add partially frozen pea pods to wok and stir in chicken until all is coated with sauce. Cover and simmer for 1 minute. Serve with rice. Sprinkle with peanuts, if desired.

PER SERVING 347 cal, 6 g fat (1 g sat. fat), 66 mg chol, 527 mg sodium, 40 g carb, 2 g fiber, 32 g pro

quick tip If you use fresh snow peas, it's a good idea to remove the strings on the flat side of the pod. Grab the string at the stem end of the pod and pull.

Snappy Chicken Stir-Fry

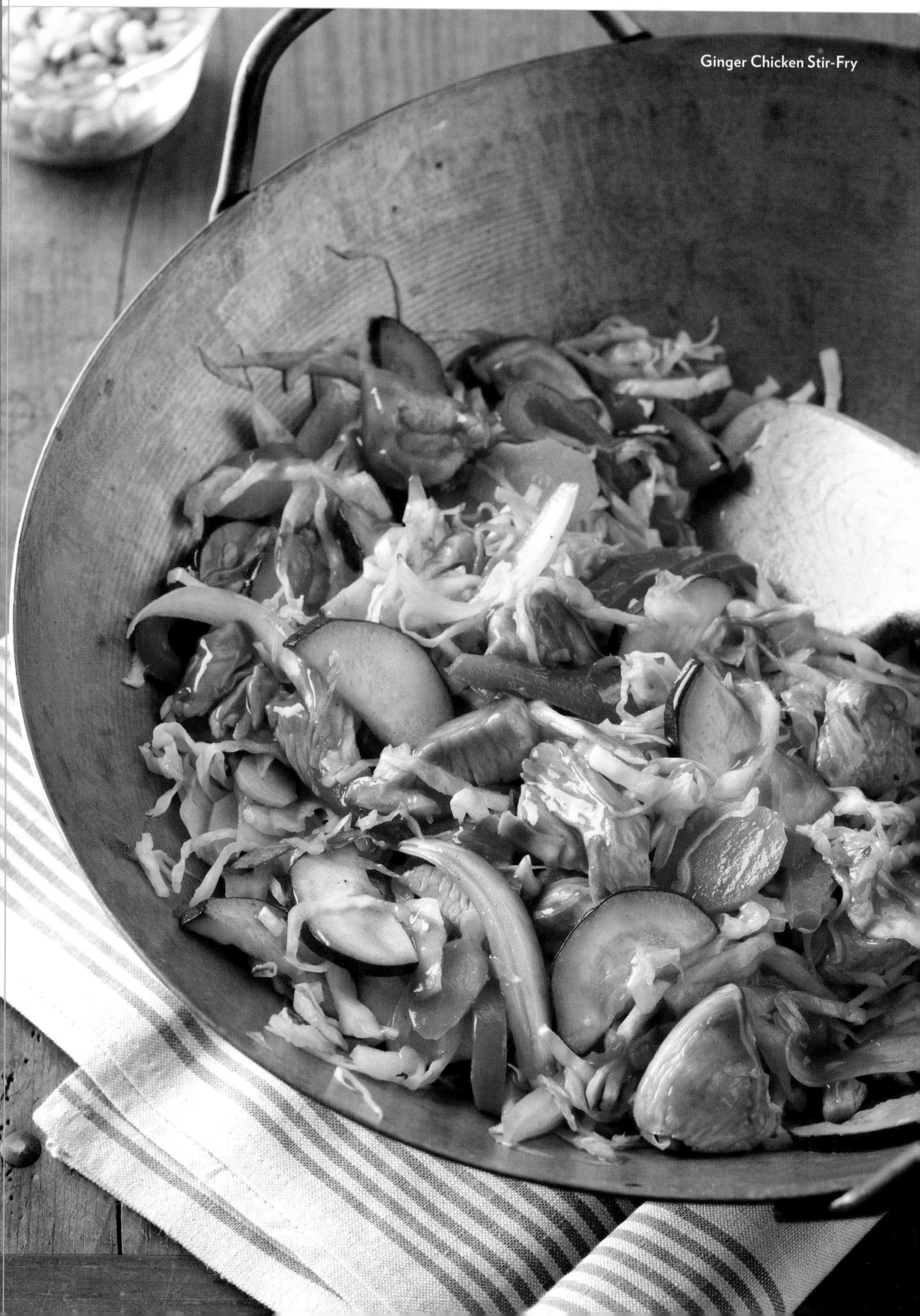

Ginger Chicken Stir-Fry

Hosin-Glazed Turkey Medallions

Nutty Turkey Tenderloins

Nutty Turkey Tenderloins

Serve these crisp-coated turkey tenderloins with sweet potatoes and steamed green beans.

MAKES 4 servings **PREP** 10 minutes **BAKE** 18 minutes
OVEN 375°F

- 2 turkey breast tenderloins (about 1 pound)
- 2 tablespoons creamy Dijon mustard blend
- ¾ cup packaged herb-seasoned or corn bread stuffing mix, crushed
- ½ cup finely chopped pecans
- 2 tablespoons butter, melted

① Preheat oven to 375°F. Split each turkey breast tenderloin in half horizontally to make 4 turkey steaks. Spread one side of each turkey steak with the mustard blend. In a shallow dish combine dry stuffing mix and pecans; dip coated side of turkey in stuffing mixture. Place turkey steaks, coated sides up, in a shallow baking pan. Sprinkle with any remaining stuffing mixture. Drizzle with melted butter.

② Bake, uncovered, for 18 to 20 minutes or until turkey is no longer pink (170°F).

PER SERVING 332 cal, 18 g fat (5 g sat. fat), 86 mg chol, 352 mg sodium, 12 g carb, 2 g fiber, 30 g pro

---

quick tip To crush stuffing mix, pour some into a resealable plastic bag. Push the air out, and seal it. Lightly roll a rolling pin over the stuffing the desired texture.

Turkey Steaks with Spinach, Pears, and Blue Cheese ♥

Pears are perfectly ripe when they are slightly fragrant and give just slightly when pressed gently. Avoid pears that have bruises or cuts.

MAKES 4 servings **START TO FINISH** 20 minutes

- 2 turkey breast tenderloins (1 to 1¼ pounds)
- 1 teaspoon dried sage, crushed
  Salt and freshly ground black pepper
- 2 tablespoons butter
- 1 6-ounce bag fresh baby spinach
- 1 large pear, cored and thinly sliced
- ¼ cup crumbled blue cheese

① Horizontally split tenderloins to make four ½-inch-thick steaks. Rub turkey with sage; sprinkle with salt and pepper. In an extra-large skillet cook steaks in 1 tablespoon of the butter over medium-high heat 14 to 16 minutes or until no longer pink (170°F), turning once. (Reduce heat to medium if turkey browns too quickly.) Remove from skillet. Add spinach to skillet. Cook and stir until just wilted.

② Meanwhile, in a small skillet cook pear slices in remaining 1 tablespoon butter over medium to medium-high heat, stirring occasionally for 5 minutes or until tender and lightly browned.

③ Serve steaks with spinach and pears. Top with blue cheese.

PER SERVING 240 cal, 9 g fat (5 g sat. fat), 92 mg chol, 380 mg sodium, 8 g carb, 2 g fiber, 31 g pro

Turkey Steaks with Spinach, Pears, and Blue Cheese

Sage-and-Cream Turkey Fettuccine ♥

The creamy sauce in this dish only tastes decadent. Made with fat-free sour cream, it has just 2 grams of fat per serving.

MAKES 2 servings **START TO FINISH** 30 minutes

- 3 ounces dried spinach and/or plain fettuccine
- ⅓ cup fat-free or light sour cream
- 2 teaspoons all-purpose flour
- ¼ cup reduced-sodium chicken broth
- 1 teaspoon snipped fresh sage or ½ teaspoon dried sage, crushed
- ⅛ teaspoon black pepper
  Nonstick cooking spray
- 6 ounces turkey breast tenderloin steak, cut into bite-size strips
- ¼ teaspoon salt
- 1 cup sliced fresh mushrooms
- 2 green onions, sliced
- 1 clove garlic, minced
  Fresh sage sprigs (optional)

① Cook pasta according to package directions; drain and set aside.

② Meanwhile, for cream sauce, in a small bowl stir together sour cream and flour until smooth. Gradually stir in broth until smooth. Stir in snipped or dried sage and pepper; set aside.

③ Coat a large unheated skillet with nonstick cooking spray. Preheat over medium-high heat. Sprinkle turkey with salt. Add turkey, mushrooms, green onions, and garlic to hot skillet. Cook and stir about 3 minutes or until turkey is no longer pink.

④ Stir cream sauce into turkey and vegetables in skillet. Cook and stir until thickened and bubbly. Cook and stir 1 minute more. Serve over hot cooked pasta. If desired, garnish with sage sprigs.

PER SERVING 312 cal, 2 g fat (0 g sat. fat), 60 mg chol, 478 mg sodium, 43 g carb, 2 g fiber, 30 g pro

Turkey Pot Pie Casserole

This recipe calls for both cooked turkey and gravy—a perfect way to put Thanksgiving leftovers to good use.

MAKES 4 servings **PREP** 15 minutes **BAKE** 10 minutes **OVEN** 450°F

- 1 16-ounce bag frozen stew vegetables (potatoes, carrots, onion, and celery)
- 1¾ cups leftover turkey gravy or one 18-ounce jar home-style gravy
- 1 teaspoon finely snipped fresh sage or ½ teaspoon ground sage
- 2 cups cooked turkey, sliced
- ¼ teaspoon black pepper
- ¼ teaspoon ground nutmeg
- 1 cooking apple, thinly sliced
  Fresh sage leaves (optional)
- 2 tablespoons butter, melted

① Preheat oven to 450°F. In a large microwave-safe bowl combine vegetables, gravy, and sage. Cover with vented plastic wrap and cook on high for 5 minutes. Add turkey, cover, and cook for 4 to 6 minutes or until heated through and vegetables are tender, stirring occasionally.

② In a small bowl combine pepper and nutmeg.

③ Spoon hot turkey into four 14- to 16-ounce individual casseroles. Top with sliced apple and, if desired, fresh sage leaves. Drizzle with melted butter and sprinkle with the nutmeg mixture.

④ Bake, uncovered, for 10 minutes or until bubbly and apples begin to brown.

PER SERVING 297 cal, 12 g fat (5 g sat. fat), 71 mg chol, 753 mg sodium, 23 g carb, 3 g fiber, 24 g pro

SEAFOOD FAVORITES

121

Sweet and Tangy Fish ♥

Be sure to get the fish fillets are dry as you can before adding them to the pan. Any moisture on the fish will make the hot oil spatter on contact.

MAKES 4 servings **START TO FINISH** 30 minutes

4	fresh or frozen skinless fish fillets (1 pound)
¾	cup chopped onion
1	tablespoon cooking oil
2	medium tomatoes, seeded and chopped (1 cup)
¾	cup frozen whole kernel corn
2	tablespoons white balsamic vinegar or white wine vinegar
1	tablespoon sugar
2	cups hot cooked couscous
¼	cup finely chopped walnuts
2	tablespoons fine dry bread crumbs
2	tablespoons snipped fresh parsley
1	tablespoon margarine or butter, melted

① Thaw fish, if frozen. Rinse fish; pat dry. Measure thickness of fillets; set aside.

② In a large skillet cook onion in hot oil until tender but not brown. Add tomatoes, corn, vinegar, and sugar. Bring to boiling. Carefully add fish fillets. Return to boiling; reduce heat. Simmer, covered, for 4 to 6 minutes per ½-inch thickness of fish or just until fish flakes with a fork.

③ To serve, place couscous on a platter; place fish on couscous. In a small bowl stir together walnuts, bread crumbs, parsley, and melted margarine; sprinkle over fish.

PER SERVING 381 cal, 13 g fat (2 g sat. fat), 53 mg chol, 162 mg sodium, 42 g carb, 5 g fiber, 26 g pro

Pan-Fried Fish ♥

Use any firm white-fleshed fish for recipe or either variation. Good choices include tilapia, or cod.

PREP 10 minutes **COOK** 6 minutes per batch
OVEN 300°F

1	pound fresh or frozen fish fillets, ½ to ¾ inch thick
1	egg, lightly beaten
2	tablespoons water
⅔	cup cornmeal or fine dry bread crumbs
½	teaspoon salt
	Dash black pepper
	Vegetable oil or shortening for frying

① Thaw fish, if frozen. Rinse fish; pat dry with paper towels. Cut into 4 serving-size pieces, if necessary. In a shallow dish combine the egg and water. In another shallow dish stir together cornmeal, salt, and pepper. Dip fish into egg mixture; coat fish with cornmeal.

② Preheat oven to 300°F. In a large skillet heat ¼ inch oil or melted shortening. Add half the fish in a single layer; fry on one side until golden. (If fillets have skin, fry skin side last.) Turn carefully. Fry until second side is golden and fish flakes when tested with a fork. Allow 3 to 4 minutes per side. Drain on paper towels. Keep warm in the preheated oven while frying remaining fish.

PER SERVING 255 cal, 13 g fat (2 g sat. fat), 101 mg chol, 230 mg sodium, 12 g carb, 1 g fiber, 23 g pro

Spicy Hot Pan-Fried Fish: Prepare as above, except omit black pepper. Reduce cornmeal to ¼ cup and combine with ¼ cup all-purpose flour, ¾ teaspoon cayenne pepper, ½ teaspoon chili powder, ½ teaspoon garlic powder, and ½ teaspoon paprika.

Potato Chip Pan-Fried Fish: Prepare as above, except substitute 1⅓ cups finely crushed potato chips (about 4 cups chips) or saltine crackers for the cornmeal and omit salt.

Sesame-Crusted Cod

Sesame-Crusted Cod ♥

Sesame seed-studded butter flavors both the fish and the green beans in this simple dish.

MAKES 4 servings **START TO FINISH** 20 minutes

- 1 pound cod fillets, ¾ inch thick
  Salt and black pepper
- 2 tablespoons sesame seeds
- 3 tablespoons butter, melted
- 1 ounce trimmed fresh tender young green beans
- 1 orange, halved and sliced
- 3 cloves garlic, thinly sliced

① Preheat broiler. Rinse cod; pat dry. Cut into 4 serving-size portions, if necessary. Place cod on the unheated rack of a broiler pan. Sprinkle cod with salt and pepper. Stir sesame seeds into the melted butter. Measure 1 tablespoon of the butter mixture and set aside for vegetables. Brush cod with half the remaining butter.

② Broil fish 5 to 6 inches from the heat for 4 minutes; turn fish. Brush with remaining half of butter. Broil 5 to 6 minutes more or until fish flakes easily when tested with a fork.

③ Meanwhile, in a very large skillet heat the reserved butter over medium-high heat. Add green beans and orange slices. Cover and cook for 2 minutes. Uncover; add garlic. Cook, uncovered, for 5 to 6 minutes more or until beans are crisp-tender, stirring frequently. Serve the beans and orange slices with cod.

PER SERVING 241 cal, 12 g fat (6 g sat. fat), 72 mg chol, 274 mg sodium, 12 g carb, 4 g fiber, 23 g pro

Steamed Cod with Gingery Mushrooms ♥

Steaming as a method of cooking is super healthful. This fish-and-veggie dish has just 155 calories and 3 grams of unsaturated fat per serving.

MAKES 4 servings **PREP** 15 minutes **COOK** 15 minutes

- 1 pound fresh or frozen skinless Alaska or gray cod, or tilapia fillets
- ½ teaspoon ground ginger
  Salt and black pepper
- 1 tablespoon finely chopped fresh ginger
- 2 teaspoons canola oil
- 8 ounces fresh shiitake mushrooms, stemmed and halved
- 1 large red sweet pepper, seeded and cut in rings
- ½ cup sliced green onions
- ¼ cup dry white wine or reduced-sodium chicken broth
- ⅔ cup reduced-sodium chicken broth
  Thin strips green onion (optional)
  Very thin slices fresh ginger (optional)

① Thaw fish, if frozen. In a bowl combine ½ teaspoon ground ginger, ¼ teaspoon salt, and ¼ teaspoon black pepper. Sprinkle on fish; set aside.

② In skillet cook 1 tablespoon fresh ginger in hot oil over medium-high heat for 15 seconds. Add mushrooms, sweet pepper, and ½ cup onions. Cook 5 minutes or until mushrooms are tender, stirring occasionally. Remove skillet from heat; add wine. Return to heat. Cook and stir until wine is almost evaporated. Add chicken broth; bring to boiling.

③ Place seasoned fish on vegetables in skillet. Reduce heat; maintain gentle boiling. Cook, covered, for 4 to 6 minutes for each ½-inch thickness of fish or until fish flakes easily when tested with fork. Serve fish and vegetables topped with onion strips and fresh ginger, if desired. Spoon cooking liquid over all.

PER SERVING 155 cal, 3 g fat (0 g sat. fat), 48 mg chol, 308 mg sodium, 6 g carb, 2 g fiber, 23 g pro

Lemon-Ginger Fish ♥

Serve this fish dish with cooked brown rice.

MAKES 4 servings **PREP** 10 minutes **COOK** 7 minutes

- 2 small lemons
- 1 tablespoon grated fresh ginger
- 2 teaspoons sugar
- 1 pound cod or other firm white fish, cut into 4 portions
- ¼ cup butter
- 2 5-ounce bags baby spinach
- ¼ teaspoon salt
- ¼ teaspoon black pepper

① Thinly slice 1 lemon; set aside. Finely shred peel from remaining lemon; juice the lemon. Add ginger, sugar, and lemon peel to the lemon juice. Set aside.

② Rinse fish and pat dry. In a large skillet melt butter over medium heat. Add fish to skillet. Cook 1 to 2 minutes or until browned. Turn fish and add lemon juice. Cover and cook 2 to 3 minutes or until tender and fish flakes easily with a fork. With a slotted spatula, transfer fish to platter; cover to keep warm.

③ Add lemon slices to the skillet. Cook for 2 minutes or until lemon slices are softened and sauce is slightly thickened.

④ Meanwhile, place spinach in a very large microwave-safe bowl. Sprinkle with 2 tablespoons water. Cook on high for 2 minutes or just until wilted, tossing once after 1 minute.

⑤ To serve, divide spinach among 4 shallow serving bowls. Top with fish and sauce. Add lemon slices and sprinkle with salt and pepper.

PER SERVING 228 cal, 12 g fat (7 g sat. fat), 79 mg chol, 344 mg sodium, 9 g carb, 3 g fiber, 22 g pro

Baked Mediterranean Cod and Asparagus ♥

While the fish is very simply cooked—dressed only with olive oil, salt, and pepper—the piquant Olive Relish packs a powerful flavor punch.

MAKES 4 servings **PREP** 15 minutes **BAKE** 12 minutes **OVEN** 475°F

- 1 recipe Olive Relish
- 2 tablespoons olive oil
- 4 cod fillets, skinned (about 1½ pounds)
  Salt and black pepper
- 1 pound asparagus, trimmed

① Prepare the Olive Relish. Preheat oven to 475°F. Lightly coat a 15 x 10 x 1-inch baking pan with some of the olive oil. On one side of pan arrange cod fillets, turning under any thin portions. Brush fish with 1 teaspoon remaining olive oil. Sprinkle with salt and pepper. Bake for 5 minutes. Place asparagus in opposite side of pan; brush with remaining olive oil; sprinkle with salt and pepper.

② Bake 7 to 10 minutes or until cod flakes easily when tested with a fork. Serve fish with Olive Relish and asparagus.

Olive Relish: In a small bowl combine ¼ cup chopped and pitted kalamata olives or pitted ripe olives; ¼ cup chopped French green olives with Herbes de Provence or pimiento-stuffed green olives; ¼ cup pepperoncini peppers (stems removed); 2 tablespoons chopped red onion; 1 tablespoon olive oil; 1 tablespoon red wine vinegar; 1 tablespoon drained capers; ½ teaspoon snipped fresh oregano or ¼ teaspoon dried oregano, crushed; and ⅛ teaspoon freshly ground black pepper. Cover and chill for 2 to 24 hours.

PER SERVING 220 cal, 9 g fat (1 g sat. fat), 73 mg chol, 309 mg sodium, 3 g carb, 2 g fiber, 32 g pro

Baked Mediterranean Cod and Asparagus

Lemon-Glazed Trout

Lemon-Glazed Trout ♥

Serve this crisp pan-fried fish with sautéed spinach.

MAKES 4 servings **START TO FINISH** 25 minutes

4	4-ounce fresh or frozen skinless trout fillets, ½ to ¾ inch thick
⅛	teaspoon salt
⅛	teaspoon black pepper
⅓	cup fat-free milk
¼	cup whole wheat flour
2	teaspoons olive oil
1	tablespoon finely chopped shallot
2	tablespoons reduced-sodium chicken broth
1	tablespoon lemon juice
2	teaspoons butter
1	tablespoon snipped fresh parsley
	Lemon wedges (optional)

① Thaw fish, if frozen. Rinse fish; pat dry with paper towels. Sprinkle fish with salt and pepper.

② Place milk in a shallow dish. Place flour in another shallow dish. Dip fish into milk, then into flour, turning to coat evenly.

③ In a large skillet heat oil over medium-high heat. Add fish; cook for 6 to 8 minutes or until golden and fish flakes easily when tested with a fork, turning once halfway through cooking. Remove fish from skillet; cover to keep warm.

④ For sauce, add shallot to the same skillet. Cook and stir over medium heat about 2 minutes or until softened. Add broth, lemon juice, and butter. Cook over low heat for 1 minute, stirring to scrape up any browned bits. Spoon sauce over fish. Sprinkle with parsley. If desired, serve with lemon wedges.

PER SERVING 240 cal, 12 g fat (3 g sat. fat), 71 mg chol, 173 mg sodium, 7 g carb, 1 g fiber, 25 g pro

Mediterranean-Style Snapper

Look for pitted mixed green olives in the olive bar of your local supermarket or specialty food store.

MAKES 4 servings **START TO FINISH** 15 minutes

4	5- to 6-ounce fresh or frozen red snapper or other fish fillets
8	small cloves garlic
½	of a 6.5-ounce jar oil-packed dried tomato halves with herbs (⅓ cup)
½	cup pitted mixed green olives
	Salt and black pepper
¼	cup crumbled feta cheese
	Fresh oregano leaves (optional)
	Pepperoncini (optional)

① Thaw fish, if frozen. Rinse fish; pat dry with paper towels. Measure thickness of fish. Set fish aside.

② Peel garlic cloves. Using the flat side of a chef's knife, smash garlic. Drain 1 tablespoon oil from dried tomatoes and pour into a very large skillet. Heat oil over medium heat. Add tomatoes, olives, and garlic; cook for 2 to 3 minutes or until garlic is golden. Using a slotted spoon; remove tomato-olive mixture and set aside.

③ Sprinkle fish with salt and pepper. Cook fish, skin side down, in hot oil until skin is golden and crisp and fish flakes easily when tested with a fork, turning once halfway through cooking. Allow 4 to 6 minutes for each ½-inch thickness of fish. If desired, remove and discard skin.

④ To serve, top fish with tomato-olive mixture and feta cheese. If desired, garnish with fresh oregano and pepperoncini.

PER SERVING 245 cal, 9 g fat (3 g sat. fat), 61 mg chol, 808 mg sodium, 8 g carb, 1 g fiber, 32 g pro

Cajun Snapper with Red Beans and Rice

The best quality frankfurters are kosher all-beef. There are several nationally distributed brands that fit this description—look for them when you make this dish.

MAKES 4 servings **START TO FINISH** 25 minutes

- 2 frankfurters, chopped
- 1 8.8-ounce package fully cooked rice
- ½ cup water
- 1 tablespoon salt-free Cajun seasoning
- 1 15 to 16-ounce can red beans, rinsed and drained
  Bottled hot pepper sauce (optional)
- 1 pound red snapper fillets, cut in 4 pieces
- 2 tablespoons butter
- 2 tablespoons all-purpose flour
  Fresh parsley (optional)

① In a medium saucepan cook frankfurters over medium heat for 2 to 3 minutes, until heated through. Stir in rice, the water, 1 teaspoon of the Cajun seasoning and the beans. Cook, covered, for 15 minutes over medium-low heat.

② Meanwhile, rinse fish; pat dry with paper towels. In a 12-inch skillet melt butter over medium heat. In a shallow dish combine flour and remaining 2 teaspoons Cajun seasoning. Press top sides of fish into the flour mixture, then place fish, skin-sides-down, in hot butter. Cook for 3 to 5 minutes, until skin is crisp. Carefully turn fish with a metal spatula. Cook for 3 to 5 minutes longer or until fish flakes easily with a fork.

③ Serve fish over rice and beans. Drizzle with pan juices and snip fresh parsley over the top.

PER SERVING 438 cal, 16 g fat (7 g sat. fat), 69 mg chol, 544 mg sodium, 41 g carb, 6 g fiber, 36 g pro

Coconut-Poached Mahi Mahi

As with all hot chiles, leave the seeds in if you like heat in your food—remove them if you don't.

MAKES 4 servings **START TO FINISH** 20 minutes

- 1 lime
- 1 15-ounce can light coconut milk
- 1 Thai green chile, thinly sliced (see note, page 47)
- 1 tablespoon sugar
- 1 pound skinless, boneless mahi mahi or other firm whitefish fillets
- 1 teaspoon salt
- 1 small head bok choy, torn (about 3 cups)
  Crystallized ginger, green chiles (optional)

① Finely shred peel from lime, then juice the lime. Set aside the peel. In a large saucepan over medium heat, combine lime juice, coconut milk, green chile, and sugar.

② Cut fish in 8 portions; rinse and pat dry with paper towels. Rub salt on fish portions, then place in coconut milk mixture in saucepan. Cook fish, covered, for 5 minutes. Uncover; gently stir in bok choy. Cook for 3 to 5 minutes more or until fish flakes easily when tested with a fork. Ladle fish with cooking liquid into bowls. Top with lime peel and, if desired, ginger and green chiles.

PER SERVING 189 cal, 7 g fat (4 g sat. fat), 83 mg chol, 744 mg sodium, 10 g carb, 1 g fiber, 22 g pro

Cajun Snapper with Red Beans and Rice

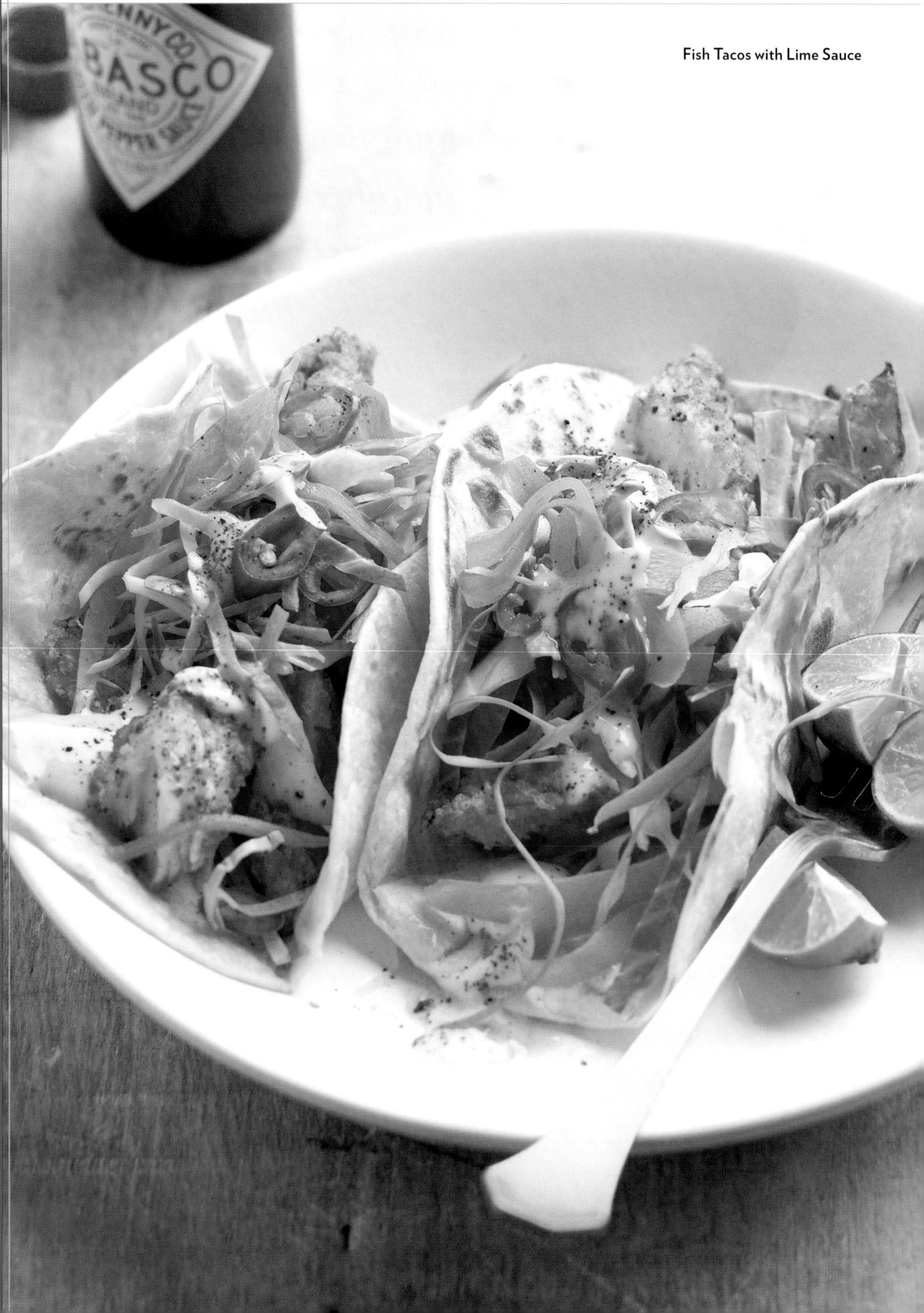

Fish Tacos with Lime Sauce

Fish Fillets with Cucumber-Orange Salsa ♥

English cucumbers are longer, slenderer, and have thinner skin than regular slicing cucumbers—and the taste is sweeter. They are virtually seedless, as well, which makes them pleasant to eat.

MAKES 4 servings **START TO FINISH** 15 minutes

- 2 6.3-ounce package frozen classic grilled salmon or classic char-grilled fish fillets
- 1 cup chopped, peeled English cucumber
- 1 large orange, peeled, seeded, and chopped
- 2 tablespoons chopped red onion
- 1 teaspoon salt-free citrus seasoning blend or garlic and herb seasoning blend

① Prepare fish according to package directions. Meanwhile, for salad, in a small bowl combine cucumber, orange, red onion, and seasoning blend. Serve with cooked fish.

PER SERVING 121 cal, 4 g fat (1 g sat. fat), 20 mg chol, 312 mg sodium, 6 g carb, 1 g fiber, 16 g pro

quick tip Frozen grilled fish fillets are offered in a wide variety of options, and are a natural source of omega-3 fatty acids.

Fish Tacos with Lime Sauce

You will get the most juice out of any citrus fruits—including limes—when they are at room temperature or slightly warm (zap them in a microwave for 10 seconds) and you roll the fruit on the counter under a flat palm a few times before cutting it in half.

MAKES 4 servings **START TO FINISH** 30 minutes

- 1 pound fresh or frozen tilapia or catfish fillets
- 3 limes
- ½ cup mayonnaise
- 1 teaspoon chili powder
- ⅓ cup all-purpose flour
- ½ teaspoon salt
- 2 tablespoons vegetable oil
- 8 taco shells or 6-inch flour tortillas, warmed
- 1 cup shredded cabbage
- ½ cup shredded carrot (1 medium)
- 1 fresh jalapeño or serrano chile pepper, thinly sliced (see note, page 47)

① Thaw fish, if frozen. Rinse fish; pat dry with paper towels. Cut fish into 1-inch pieces.

② For sauce, juice 2 of the limes into a small bowl; cut the remaining lime into wedges and reserve for serving. Stir mayonnaise and chili powder into lime juice. Transfer ⅓ cup of the sauce to a medium bowl. Add fish; toss gently to coat.

③ In a shallow dish combine flour and salt. Dip fish in flour mixture, turning to coat. In a large skillet heat oil over medium heat. Cook fish, about one-third at a time, in hot oil for 2 to 4 minutes or until fish flakes easily when tested with a fork, turning to brown evenly and adding more oil as necessary during cooking. Drain on paper towels.

④ Fill taco shells (if using) with fish, cabbage, carrot, and jalapeño pepper. (If using tortillas, lay each tortilla on a flat surface; sprinkle ingredients in center. Fold sides over filling.) Serve with the remaining sauce and reserved lime wedges.

PER SERVING 652 cal, 39 g fat (5 g sat. fat), 67 mg chol, 557 mg sodium, 41 g carb, 2 g fiber, 31 g pro

Catfish and Slaw Tacos

If you don't have Cajun seasoning, make some. For 1 tablespoon, combine ½ teaspoon each white pepper, garlic powder, onion powder, cayenne pepper, paprika, and black pepper.

MAKES 8 tacos **START TO FINISH** 30 minutes

1	pound fresh or frozen catfish fillets
¼	cup mayonnaise
3	tablespoons lime juice
½	teaspoon bottled hot pepper sauce
2½	cups shredded cabbage (half of a small head)
1	tablespoon Cajun seasoning
¼	cup cornmeal
¼	cup all-purpose flour
¼	cup vegetable oil
16	4-inch corn tortillas or eight 8-inch flour tortillas
	Lime wedges
	Bottled hot pepper sauce

① Thaw fish, if frozen. Rinse fish; pat dry with paper towels. Cut fish into 1-inch strips; set fish aside.

② For slaw, in a medium bowl combine mayonnaise, lime juice, and ½ teaspoon hot pepper sauce. Add cabbage; toss to coat. Set slaw aside.

③ Toss fish strips with Cajun seasoning. In a large bowl combine cornmeal and flour. Add fish strips; toss to coat.

④ In a large skillet heat oil over medium heat. Cook fish strips, half at a time, in hot oil for 4 to 6 minutes or until golden and fish flakes easily when tested with a fork, turning to brown evenly. Remove from skillet.

⑤ Wrap tortillas in paper towels. Heat in microwave oven on high for 1 minute. If using corn tortillas, stack 2 for each taco, or use 1 flour tortilla for each taco. Divide fish and slaw among tortillas. Reserve any dressing in bowl to serve with tacos. Serve tacos immediately with reserved dressing, lime wedges, and additional hot pepper sauce.

PER TACO 620 cal, 36 g fat (5 g sat. fat), 59 mg chol, 300 mg sodium, 53 g carb, 3 g fiber, 24 g pro

Crisp Catfish with Apple-Celery Slaw

If you don't like the strings on celery, drag a vegetable peeler along the back of the stalk to remove them.

MAKES 4 servings **START TO FINISH** 25 minutes

1	lemon
⅓	cup mayonnaise
1	tablespoon honey
3	stalks celery, thinly sliced
1	Granny Smith apple, thinly sliced
1	cup shredded red cabbage
1	to 1½ pounds catfish fillets
½	teaspoon salt
⅓	cup yellow cornmeal
1	teaspoon chili powder
2	tablespoon vegetable oil

① Cut half of lemon in slices or wedges; set aside. Juice remaining half into a large bowl. For slaw, combine mayonnaise and honey with lemon juice; reserve 2 tablespoons and set aside. Stir celery, apple, and cabbage into juice in bowl; set aside.

② Sprinkle catfish fillets with salt and brush with reserved juice. In shallow dish combine cornmeal and chili powder; coat fish with mixture.

③ In a large skillet heat oil over medium heat. Cook fish in hot oil 3 to 4 minutes per side until golden and fish flakes easily with a fork. Serve fish with slaw and lemon.

PER SERVING 446 cal, 31 g fat (5 g sat. fat), 60 mg chol, 488 mg sodium, 25 g carb, 4 g fiber, 19 g pro

Spice-Rubbed Salmon

As it grills, the brown sugar-and-spice rub creates a crisp, caramelized crust on the salmon, which stays juicy and buttery-tasting in the center.

MAKES 4 servings **START TO FINISH** 20 minutes

- 2 teaspoons chili powder
- 1 teaspoon ground cumin
- 1 teaspoon packed brown sugar
  Salt and black pepper
- 4 5-ounce skinless salmon fillets
- 1 small cabbage, cut in 6 wedges
- 2 to 3 tablespoons cooking oil
- 1 large carrot
  Orange wedges

① In a small bowl mix chili powder, cumin, brown sugar, ¼ teaspoon salt, and ⅛ teaspoon black pepper. Rub spice mixture on salmon. Brush cabbage wedges with 1 tablespoon of the oil.

② For a charcoal grill, place salmon and cabbage on greased rack of uncovered grill, directly over medium coals. Grill salmon 4 to 6 minutes for each half-inch of thickness or until it flakes when tested with a fork, turning once halfway through cooking time. Grill cabbage 6 to 8 minutes, turning once. (For a gas grill, preheat grill. Reduce heat to medium. Place salmon and cabbage on grill rack over heat. Cover and grill as above.)

③ Meanwhile, peel carrot and cut in wide strips. Remove fish and cabbage from grill. Coarsely cut cabbage; combine with carrot and 1 to 2 tablespoons remaining oil. Season with salt and pepper. Serve with oranges.

PER SERVING 380 cal, 23 g fat (4 g sat. fat), 84 mg chol, 284 mg sodium, 14 g carb, 5 g fiber, 31 g pro

Simple Grilled Salmon with Kalamata-Orange Relish

Smoked paprika comes two ways—sweet (mild) and hot. If you like spicy flavors, try the "picante" or hot variety in place of the "dulce," or sweet stuff. Or try a half teaspoon of each. Stir the two together in a small bowl before sprinkling on the salmon.

MAKES 4 servings **START TO FINISH** 30 minutes

- 4 6-ounce skinless salmon fillets
- 2 tablespoons olive oil
- 1 teaspoon smoked paprika
  Salt and black pepper
- 3 medium oranges
- ½ cup kalamata pitted olives, coarsely chopped
- ½ cup chopped red sweet pepper

① Lightly grease a grill pan. Heat grill pan over medium heat. Brush salmon with 1 tablespoon of the oil. Sprinkle with smoked paprika, salt, and pepper. Place salmon on grill pan. Cook 4 to 6 minutes per ½-inch thickness of fish, or until fish flakes when tested with a fork, turning once halfway through grilling.

② Meanwhile, for relish, finely shred 1 teaspoon of peel from one orange. Peel and dice oranges. In a medium bowl combine oranges, orange peel, olives, red sweet pepper, and remaining 1 tablespoon olive oil. Serve salmon with relish.

PER SERVING 493 cal, 32 g fat (6 g sat. fat), 94 mg chol, 580 mg sodium, 15 g carb, 4 g fiber, 36 g pro

Shrimp and Tomatoes with Pasta

To devein shrimp after peeling, make a shallow cut along the rounded side of the shrimp with the point of a sharp paring knife. Rinse out the vein under cool running water.

MAKES 4 servings **START TO FINISH** 25 minutes

- 1 9-ounce package refrigerated fettuccine
- 12 ounces fresh or frozen uncooked, peeled, and deveined shrimp, thawed
- 2 tablespoons olive oil or cooking oil
- ½ cup chopped onion (1 medium)
- 1 medium green sweet pepper, cut into thin bite-size strips
- 1 14.5-ounce can diced tomatoes with basil, garlic, and oregano, undrained
- ¼ teaspoon black pepper
- ¼ cup finely shredded Parmesan cheese (1 ounce)

① Using kitchen scissors, cut fettuccine strands in half. In a 4-quart Dutch oven cook shrimp with the fettuccine according to fettuccine package directions until pasta is tender and shrimp are opaque. Drain. Return to the hot pan.

② Meanwhile, in a large skillet heat oil over medium-high heat. Add onion; cook for 2 minutes. Add sweet pepper strips; cook and stir for 2 to 3 minutes or until onion is tender. Stir in undrained tomatoes and black pepper. Bring to boiling; reduce heat. Simmer, uncovered, for 2 minutes.

③ Add tomato mixture to fettuccine mixture; toss to combine. Sprinkle individual servings with Parmesan cheese.

PER SERVING 406 cal, 12 g fat (3 g sat. fat), 174 mg chol, 758 mg sodium, 47 g carb, 3 g fiber, 29 g pro

Shrimp with Peppers and Corn

For extra flavor, serve this colorful dish with salsa verde or green chile-hot sauce.

MAKES 4 servings **START TO FINISH** 25 minutes

- 1 8.8-ounce pouch cooked long grain rice
- 1 14.5-ounce can diced tomatoes with chili seasoning
   Salt and black pepper
- ½ teaspoon ground cumin
- 2 tablespoons olive oil or butter
- 1 cup sliced baby or diced sweet peppers
- 1 cup frozen whole kernel corn, thawed
- 2 cloves garlic, minced
- 1 pound peeled and deveined medium raw shrimp
   Fresh parsley

① In a small saucepan combine rice and undrained tomatoes. In a small bowl mix together ½ teaspoon each salt and pepper with the cumin; stir half into the rice. Cover and cook over medium heat until heated through. Reduce heat to low; cover and keep warm.

② Meanwhile, in a very large skillet heat oil over medium-high heat. Add peppers and corn. Cook, stirring occasionally, for 3 to 4 minutes. Stir in garlic. Sprinkle shrimp with remaining salt-cumin mixture. Add shrimp to skillet. Cook until shrimp are opaque and peppers are crisp tender (2 to 5 minutes, depending on size of shrimp).

③ Serve over rice; sprinkle with parsley.

PER SERVING 355 cal, 11 g fat (1 g sat. fat), 172 mg chol, 944 mg sodium, 38 g carb, 4 g fiber, 27 g pro

Pepper Shrimp in Peanut Sauce

Creamy Shrimp and Spinach Stew

Gruyère cheese is a fairly strong flavor cheese with nutty taste and aroma. It can be pricey. Substitute Swiss cheese if you prefer.

MAKES 4 servings **START TO FINISH** 30 minutes

8	ounces fresh or frozen, peeled, deveined small shrimp
1	cup sliced fresh mushrooms
½	cup onion, chopped (1 medium)
1	clove garlic, minced
2	tablespoons margarine or butter
3	tablespoons all-purpose flour
1	bay leaf
⅛	teaspoon ground nutmeg
⅛	teaspoon black pepper
1	14.5-ounce can vegetable or chicken broth
1	cup half-and-half, light cream, or milk
2	cups torn fresh spinach
¾	cup shredded Gruyère cheese (3 ounces)

① Thaw shrimp, if frozen. Rinse shrimp; set aside.

② In a medium saucepan cook mushrooms, onion, and garlic in margarine until tender. Stir in flour, bay leaf, nutmeg, and pepper. Add broth and half-and-half all at once. Cook and stir until thickened and bubbly.

③ Add shrimp. Cook for 2 minutes. Add spinach and Gruyère cheese. Cook and stir until spinach is wilted and cheese is melted. Remove and discard bay leaf.

PER SERVING 370 cal, 22 g fat (10 g sat. fat), 135 mg chol, 965 mg sodium, 22 g carb, 22 g pro

Creamy Shrimp and Spinach Stew

Pepper Shrimp in Peanut Sauce

Slicing the green onions on the bias simply means to cut them on an angle. (They're prettier that way!)

MAKES 4 servings **START TO FINISH** 30 minutes

1	pound fresh or frozen shrimp in shells
8	ounces farfalle (bow tie pasta) or linguine or 1 cup long grain rice
½	cup water
¼	cup orange marmalade
2	tablespoons peanut butter
2	tablespoons soy sauce
2	teaspoons cornstarch
¼	teaspoon crushed red pepper
1	tablespoon cooking oil
2	medium red, yellow, and/or green sweet peppers, cut into strips (about 2½ cups)
6	green onions, bias-sliced into 1-inch pieces
	Chopped peanuts (optional)

① Thaw shrimp, if frozen. Peel and devein shrimp; rinse and pat dry. Set aside.

② Cook pasta according to package directions; drain.

③ Meanwhile, for sauce, in a small bowl stir together the water, orange marmalade, peanut butter, soy sauce, cornstarch, and crushed red pepper. Set aside.

④ Pour cooking oil into a wok or large skillet. (Add more oil as necessary during cooking.) Preheat on medium-high heat. Add pepper strips and green onions; stir-fry for 1 to 2 minutes or until crisp-tender. Remove and set aside.

⑤ Add half the shrimp to wok; stir-fry for 2 to 3 minutes or until shrimp turn opaque; remove and set aside. Cook remaining shrimp.

⑥ Stir sauce; add to center of wok. Cook and stir until thickened and bubbly. Cook and stir for 2 minutes more. Remove from heat; keep sauce warm.

⑦ In a 4-quart Dutch oven combine cooked pasta, vegetables, and shrimp; cook over medium heat until heated through, tossing gently to mix. Serve on dinner plates. Top with sauce. If desired, sprinkle with chopped peanuts.

PER SERVING 435 cal, 9 g fat (2 g sat. fat), 131 mg chol, 710 mg sodium, 64 g carb, 24 g pro

Shrimp Scampi

A squeeze of fresh lemon right before serving is the perfect complement to the richness of the garlicky butter sauce in this classic shrimp dish.

MAKES 4 servings **START TO FINISH** 20 minutes

1½	pounds fresh or frozen large shrimp
8	ounces dried angel hair pasta
¼	cup butter, melted
¼	cup olive oil
6	cloves garlic, minced
¼	teaspoon salt
⅛	teaspoon crushed red pepper
2	tablespoons snipped fresh parsley
1	teaspoon finely shredded lemon peel
	Lemon wedges (optional)

① Thaw shrimp, if frozen. Peel and devein shrimp, leaving tails intact, if desired. Rinse shrimp; pat dry with paper towels. Set shrimp aside.

② In a large pot cook pasta according to package directions; drain. Return pasta to pot.

③ Meanwhile, in a large skillet heat butter, olive oil, and garlic over medium-high heat. Add shrimp, salt, and crushed red pepper to skillet. Cook and stir about 3 minutes or until shrimp are opaque. Stir in parsley and lemon peel. Add shrimp to pasta; toss to combine. If desired, serve with lemon wedges.

PER SERVING 574 cal, 28 g fat (10 g sat. fat), 224 mg chol, 390 mg sodium, 45 g carb, 1 g fiber, 33 g pro

Shrimp, Chickpea, and Feta Cheese Nests 🍲

Make a nest by twirling the spaghetti with a fork after it's been plated, then pretty it up with lemon wedges, green olives, and a drizzle of extra-virgin olive oil.

MAKES 8 servings **START TO FINISH** 30 minutes

1	16-ounce package dried multigrain, whole wheat, or regular spaghetti
2	15- to 16-ounce cans chickpeas (garbanzo beans), rinsed and drained
1	16-ounce bag frozen peeled, cooked shrimp with tails, thawed
3	roma tomatoes, seeded and chopped
1	cup feta cheese, crumbled (4 ounces)
2	tablespoons chopped fresh mint
1	teaspoon finely shredded lemon peel
2	tablespoons lemon juice
1	teaspoon dried oregano, crushed
	Salt and black pepper
	Lemon wedges
	Green olives (optional)
	Olive oil

① Cook spaghetti, with 1 tablespoon salt added to water, according to package directions; add drained chickpeas and shrimp during the last 1 minute of pasta cooking time. Drain.

② Return pasta mixture to pan. Stir in tomatoes, cheese, mint, lemon peel, lemon juice, oregano, and ¼ teaspoon each salt and black pepper.

③ Serve with lemon wedges and, if desired, green olives. Drizzle with olive oil.

PER SERVING 696 cal, 14 g fat (3 g sat. fat), 123 mg chol, 408 mg sodium, 102 g carb, 23 g fiber, 44 g pro

Basil-Lemon Shrimp Linguine

Scallop Salad with Basil Vinaigrette

Scallop Salad with Basil Vinaigrette ♥

There are two basic types of scallops—bay scallops and sea scallops. Sea scallops are the larger of the two. Be sure to pat the scallops as dry as possible with paper towels. The drier the scallops before cooking, the better the sear (which produces the lovely crust).

MAKES 4 servings **START TO FINISH** 25 minutes

- 1 pound fresh or frozen sea scallops
- ¼ cup snipped fresh basil
- 3 tablespoons balsamic vinegar
- 2 tablespoons lemon juice
- 2 tablespoons olive oil
- 2 teaspoons Dijon mustard
- ½ teaspoon black pepper
  Nonstick cooking spray
- 6 cups torn mixed salad greens
- 3 roma tomatoes, seeded and chopped
- 1 medium red sweet pepper, seeded and chopped
- 1 cup fresh corn kernels or frozen whole kernel corn, thawed
- ½ of a medium English cucumber, chopped
- 2 tablespoons finely shredded Parmesan cheese (optional)

① Thaw scallops, if frozen. Rinse scallops; pat dry with paper towels. For vinaigrette, in a screw-top jar combine basil, vinegar, lemon juice, oil, mustard, and ¼ teaspoon of the black pepper. Cover and shake well. Set aside.

② Sprinkle scallops with the remaining ¼ teaspoon black pepper. Coat an large unheated nonstick skillet with cooking spray. Preheat over medium-high heat. Add scallops. Cook for 2 to 4 minutes or until scallops are opaque, turning once halfway through cooking.

③ Meanwhile, divide salad greens among 4 serving plates. In a large bowl combine tomatoes, sweet pepper, corn, and cucumber. Add half the vinaigrette; toss to coat. Add to serving plates with greens. Add scallops to salads and brush with some of the remaining vinaigrette. Pass the remaining vinaigrette. If desired, sprinkle with Parmesan cheese.

PER SERVING 256 cal, 9 g fat (1 g sat. fat), 37 mg chol, 241 mg sodium, 22 g carb, 4 g fiber, 23 g pro

Gazpacho Crab and Pasta Salad ♥

For even more zing, use the spicy-hot version of the low-sodium vegetable juice in the Spicy Tomato Dressing.

MAKES 4 servings **PREP** 20 minutes **CHILL** 1 hour

- 5 ounces dried whole grain medium shell macaroni (about 1½ cups)
- 1 recipe Spicy Tomato Dressing
- 2 medium tomatoes, seeded and chopped (1 cup)
- 1 cup chopped cucumber
- ½ cup small red sweet pepper, chopped (1 small)
- ½ cup green sweet pepper, chopped (1 small)
- ⅓ cup slivered red onion
- ¼ cup snipped fresh cilantro
- 6 ounces cooked crab meat, flaked, or 8 ounces cooked peeled small shrimp

① Cook pasta according to package directions; rinse with cold water and drain.

② In a large bowl combine pasta, Spicy Tomato Dressing, tomatoes, cucumber, sweet peppers, onion, and cilantro; toss to coat. Gently stir in crab meat. Chill for 1 hour or until ready to serve. To serve, divide salad among 4 serving plates.

Spicy Tomato Dressing: In a screw-top jar combine 1 cup low-sodium vegetable juice; 1 tablespoon olive oil; 1 tablespoon red wine vinegar; 1 clove garlic, minced; 1 teaspoon smoked paprika; and ¼ teaspoon cayenne pepper. Cover and shake well until combined.

PER SERVING 238 cal, 5 g fat (1 g sat. fat), 38 mg chol, 282 mg sodium, 36 g carb, 3 g fiber, 12 g pro

quick tip If pasta absorbs dressing while chilling, add a little more low-sodium vegetable juice to moisten it.

These scrumptious, savory dishes featuring vegetables, cheese, grains, and pasta allow health-conscious eaters—or vegetarians—to cut back on (or eliminate) meat without sacrificing flavor.

128

135

148

MEATLESS MAIN DISHES

135

Cumin-Crusted Veggie Burgers with Pineapple Salsa

If you like fresh pineapple but don't want to mess with cutting up a whole one, look for the cored and peeled fresh pineapples in the produce section of your supermarket.

MAKES 4 burgers **START TO FINISH** 20 minutes

- 2 teaspoons cumin seeds
- 4 refrigerated or frozen meatless burger patties, thawed
- 6 slices fresh or canned pineapple
  Olive oil
- 4 pita breads or flatbreads
- 1 tablespoon bottled pepper and onion relish
  Spiced peanuts and fresh basil (optional)

① In a medium skillet heat cumin seeds over medium heat until they are fragrant and starting to brown, about 3 to 4 minutes. Transfer to a cutting board. Crush seeds using a mortar and pestle or with a rolling pin.

② Brush meatless patties with olive oil; coat with crushed cumin seeds. Blot excess moisture from pineapple slices and lightly coat with olive oil.

③ Grill pineapple slices directly over medium-high heat for 3 to 4 minutes per side or until heated through. Transfer to a cutting board. Add meatless patties to grill; cook 4 minutes per side or until heated through, adding pita breads the last 3 to 4 minutes of grilling. Cover and keep warm.

④ For salsa, chop pineapple and place in a bowl; stir in relish.

⑤ Serve veggie burgers on pita bread with salsa and, if desired, spiced peanuts and basil.

PER BURGER 316 cal, 5 g fat (1 g sat. fat), 0 mg chol, 619 mg sodium, 52 g carb, 6 g fiber, 19 g pro

Bruschetta Burgers

To shred basil, stack the leaves then roll them up. Use a small, thin paring knife to cut the roll in thin slices. (In French terms, this is a chiffonade.)

MAKES 4 burgers **START TO FINISH** 25 minutes

- 1 package frozen tomato-, basil-, and Parmesan cheese-flavor meatless burger patties
- 4 slices mozzarella cheese (about 3 ounces total)
- 2 thin multigrain sandwich rounds or 4 slices whole wheat bread
- 8 to 12 fresh basil leaves
- 4 slices tomato
  Shredded fresh basil (optional)

① Prepare frozen patties according to package directions. Arrange patties on one side on a large baking sheet. Top with cheese slices. Separate sandwich rounds and place, cut sides up, on the baking sheet with the patties.

② Broil 4 to 5 inches from the heat for 1 to 2 minutes or until cheese is melted and sandwich rounds are toasted. Divide basil leaves among sandwich rounds. Top each with a patty and a tomato slice. If desired, top with shredded basil.

PER BURGER 178 cal, 5 g fat (3 g sat. fat), 16 mg chol, 538 mg sodium, 21 g carb, 6 g fiber, 17 g pro

quick tip If you like, dress up this Italian-inspired burger with pesto mayo. Combine about 2 teaspoons pesto with 2 tablespoons low-fat mayonnaise. Spread one-quarter of the mixture on each of the buns.

 With so many choices for meatless patties on the market, a juicy burger can taste good and be good for you.

Bruschetta Burgers

Black Bean Tostadas

Grilled Vegetables on Ciabatta

This yummy sandwich—with grilled veggies and creamy goat-cheese spread—is much like the vegetarian grilled sandwiches in fancy restaurants.

MAKES 6 servings **START TO FINISH** 30 minutes

- 3 tablespoons red wine vinegar
- 2 tablespoons water
- 1 tablespoon olive oil
- 1 teaspoon dried oregano, crushed
- ¼ teaspoon salt
- ¼ teaspoon black pepper
- 3 red and/or orange sweet peppers
- 2 zucchini and/or yellow summer squash, halved crosswise and sliced lengthwise into ¼-inch slices
- 1 pound purchased ciabatta bread
- 2 ounces soft goat cheese (chèvre)
- 2 ounces reduced-fat cream cheese (Neufchâtel), softened
  Fresh oregano (optional)

① In a small bowl whisk together vinegar, the water, oil, dried oregano, salt, and black pepper. Set aside. Cut sweet peppers into quarters. Remove stems, membranes, and seeds. Brush sweet pepper quarters and zucchini slices with some of the vinegar mixture.

② For a charcoal grill, grill vegetables on the rack of an uncovered grill directly over medium coals until crisp-tender, turning once halfway through grilling and brushing often with the vinegar mixture. Allow 8 to 10 minutes for sweet peppers and 5 to 6 minutes for zucchini. Remove vegetables from grill. (For a gas grill, preheat grill. Reduce heat to medium. Place vegetables on grill rack. Cover and grill as above.) Cut peppers into strips.

③ Halve ciabatta lengthwise. Place ciabatta halves, cut sides down, directly over medium coals for 1 to 2 minutes or until bread is lightly toasted. In a small bowl combine goat cheese and cream cheese, stirring until smooth.

④ To assemble, spread cheese on bottom half of the ciabatta. Top with sweet peppers and zucchini. Drizzle with any remaining vinegar mixture. Place the top half of the ciabatta on vegetables. Slice to serve. If desired, garnish with fresh oregano.

PER SERVING 312 cal, 9 g fat (4 g sat. fat), 12 mg chol, 621 mg sodium, 45 g carb, 5 g fiber, 11 g pro

Black Bean Tostadas ♥

This no-cook recipe is so quick to fix, you can make it for an eat-and-run lunch.

MAKES 4 servings **START TO FINISH** 20 minutes

- 1 16-ounce can no-salt-added black beans, rinsed and drained
- ½ cup canned fat-free refried beans
- ½ teaspoon ground cumin
- ½ teaspoon chili powder
- 4 tostada shells
- 1 cup shredded lettuce
- ¾ cup diced tomatoes
- ¼ cup shredded reduced-fat cheddar cheese
- 2 tablespoons fat-free sour cream
- 2 tablespoons snipped fresh cilantro

① In a medium bowl use a potato masher to coarsely mash together black beans, refried beans, cumin, and chili powder. Spread on tostada shells. Sprinkle with lettuce, tomatoes, and cheese. Spoon sour cream on and sprinkle with cilantro.

PER SERVING 218 cal, 9 g fat (2 g sat. fat), 5 mg chol, 253 mg sodium, 22 g carb, 9 g fiber, 14 g pro

quick tip If you like beans warm, heat them in the microwave for 1 minute before spreading on the tostada shells.

Bean Burritos with Lime Mayonnaise

A simple salad of shredded lettuce and halved cherry tomatoes tossed in a quick lime mayonnaise adds color and crunch to these meatless burritos.

MAKES 4 servings **START TO FINISH** 20 minutes

- 4 8- to 10-inch flour tortillas
- 1 16-ounce can refried beans
- ¼ cup salsa
- ¼ cup mayonnaise or salad dressing
- ½ teaspoon finely shredded lime peel
- 1 tablespoon lime juice
- 2 cups shredded lettuce
- ½ cup cherry tomatoes, quartered
- ½ cup Monterey Jack cheese with jalapeño chile peppers, shredded (2 ounces)

① Place tortillas between paper towels. Microwave on high for 20 to 30 seconds or until heated through.

② Meanwhile, in a small saucepan combine refried beans and salsa. Cook over medium heat until heated through, stirring frequently.

③ In a medium bowl combine mayonnaise, lime peel, and lime juice. Add lettuce and tomatoes; toss to coat.

④ Spoon about ½ cup of the bean mixture onto each tortilla just below the center. Top each with 2 tablespoons cheese and about ⅓ cup of the lettuce mixture. Roll up tortillas.

PER SERVING 414 cal, 19 g fat (6 g sat. fat), 29 mg chol, 992 mg sodium, 47 g carb, 9 g fiber, 15 g pro

Bean Burritos with Lime Mayonnaise

Tofu Stackup

To be sure that the tofu fries as crispy as possible, remove as much water as you can from it. Layer slices between clean paper towels and weight them few minutes with a dinner plate before coating the with the cornmeal.

MAKES 4 servings **START TO FINISH** 30 minutes

- 2 ears fresh sweet corn
- 2 12- to 16-ounce package firm or extra-firm tofu, drained
- ⅓ cup yellow cornmeal
- 2 teaspoons chili powder
- ½ teaspoon salt
- 3 to 4 tablespoons olive oil
- 1 medium red sweet pepper, seeded and sliced
- 2 medium green tomatoes, sliced
  Lime wedges
  Fresh cilantro leaves (optional)

① In a large saucepan cook corn, covered, in boiling salted water for 7 minutes. Drain.

② Meanwhile, cut each block of tofu horizontally into 4 slices. In a shallow dish combine cornmeal, chili powder, and salt; dip tofu into mixture to coat.

③ In a large skillet heat 1 tablespoon of the oil over medium-high heat. Cook tofu in batches for 2 to 3 minutes per side until crisp and golden brown, adding more oil as needed. Remove tofu from skillet; add sweet pepper and green tomatoes and cook in remaining oil about 3 minutes until tomatoes are heated through and lightly browned and peppers are crisp tender.

④ Cut corn from cob. Place 1 slice tofu on each of 4 serving plates. Top with half the corn, peppers, and tomatoes. Top with remaining tofu slices, and remaining corn, peppers, and tomatoes. Serve with lime wedges and, if desired, fresh cilantro leaves.

PER SERVING 306 cal, 16 g fat (2 g sat. fat), 0 mg chol, 382 mg sodium, 28 g carb, 4 g fiber, 15 g pro

Corn and Bean Fritters with Tomatoes

Broccoli Spaghetti

A topping of crushed croutons gives this pasta dish surprisingly pleasant crunch.

MAKES 4 servings **START TO FINISH** 25 minutes

- 6 ounces dried spaghetti
- 3 cups broccoli florets
- 1 15- to 19-ounce can cannellini beans (white kidney beans), rinsed and drained
- 1 10-ounce container refrigerated light Alfredo sauce
- 3 cloves garlic, minced
- ½ cup croutons, coarsely crushed
- ¼ teaspoon crushed red pepper
  Olive oil

① Cook pasta according to package directions, adding broccoli the last 3 to 4 minutes of cooking; drain, reserving ½ cup of the cooking water. Return pasta to hot pan; keep warm.

② Meanwhile, for sauce in a blender or food processor combine beans, Alfredo sauce, garlic, and the reserved cooking water; cover and blend or process until nearly smooth. Transfer to a small saucepan; heat through over medium heat, stirring frequently.

③ Spoon sauce onto serving plates. Top with pasta and broccoli, crushed croutons, and crushed red pepper. Drizzle with olive oil.

PER SERVING 402 cal, 12 g fat (5 g sat. fat), 18 mg chol, 659 mg sodium, 60 g carb, 8 g fiber, 19 g pro

Quick Vegetable Pasta with Provolone ♥

This dish made with itty-bitty pasta, finely chopped veggies, and tiny cubes of cheese will be a hit with kids. It's a fun way to get them to eat and love vegetables.

MAKES 4 servings **START TO FINISH** 30 minutes

- 1 cup dried small alphabet-shape pasta, acini de pepe, or large couscous
- 1½ cups assorted vegetables, such as finely chopped carrots, red sweet pepper, and broccoli and/or frozen baby peas, edamame, and whole kernel corn
- 1 tablespoon olive oil
- ⅛ teaspoon black pepper
- ⅓ cup finely chopped provolone or cheddar cheese

① In a large saucepan cook pasta according to package directions, adding vegetables the last 5 minutes of cooking; drain. Return pasta and vegetables to hot saucepan.

② Add oil and pepper to pasta mixture; toss gently to coat. Cool slightly. Add cheese; toss gently to combine.

PER SERVING 314 cal, 8 g fat (3 g sat. fat), 11 mg chol, 159 mg sodium, 47 g carb, 3 g fiber, 12 g pro

 Versatile and popular pasta is a go-to meatless meal.

Asian Noodle Slaw ♥

This peanut-sauced noodle slaw is served warm the first time. Leftovers can be refrigerated and eaten cool or at room temperature for lunch the next day.

MAKES 4 servings **START TO FINISH** 25 minutes

- 6 ounces multigrain spaghetti or soba (buckwheat) noodles
- ⅓ cup peanut sauce
- ⅓ cup carrot juice
- 1 tablespoon finely chopped, peeled fresh ginger
- 1 tablespoon canola oil
- 1 16-ounce package shredded broccoli (broccoli slaw mix)
- ¾ cup shredded carrots

① Cook noodles according to package directions; drain. Return to pan. Using kitchen scissors, snip noodles into small pieces. Cover and keep warm. In a bowl whisk together peanut sauce and carrot juice; set aside.

② In a wok or nonstick skillet stir-fry ginger in hot oil over medium-high heat for 15 seconds. Add broccoli slaw and carrots. Cook and stir for 1 minute.

③ Add peanut sauce mixture to skillet. Stir to coat vegetables. Cook and stir 2 minutes more. Add noodles. Using tongs, toss to coat. Serve warm.

PER SERVING 285 cal, 7 g fat (1 g sat. fat), 0 mg chol, 318 mg sodium, 45 g carb, 7 g fiber, 12 g pro

Asian Noodle Slaw

Linguine with Green Beans and Goat Cheese

Leeks can harbor grit and dirt in the layers. To clean, slice (white part only), then swirl the slices in a bowl of cool water. Drain and repeat, then pat dry with clean paper towels. (Alternately, swirl them in a salad spinner and spin dry.)

MAKES 6 servings **PREP** 15 minutes **COOK** 13 minutes

- 12 cups water
- ½ teaspoon salt
- 8 ounces dried linguine or spaghetti
- 1 9-ounce package frozen cut green beans
- 2 medium leeks, thinly sliced (about ⅔ cup)
- ½ cup chopped walnuts
- 2 tablespoons olive oil
- 1 tablespoon butter or margarine
- 1 tablespoon snipped fresh thyme or marjoram
- 4 ounces semisoft goat cheese (chèvre), crumbled
  Cracked black pepper

① Bring the water and salt to boiling in a 4-quart Dutch oven. Add pasta; boil for 5 minutes. Add green beans. Continue boiling, uncovered, about 5 minutes more or until pasta is tender but still firm. Drain in a colander and set aside.

② Cook leeks and walnuts in hot olive oil and butter in the same Dutch oven for 3 to 4 minutes or until leeks are tender and walnuts are lightly toasted. Stir in drained pasta and beans and thyme; heat through. Transfer to a serving platter. Sprinkle with cheese and pepper. Serve immediately.

PER SERVING 351 cal, 19 g fat (6 g sat. fat), 20 mg chol, 125 mg sodium, 35 g carb, 3 g fiber, 11 g pro

Roma Tomato and Feta Pasta Toss

Roma Tomato and Feta Pasta Toss

Use one of the flavored feta cheeses in this Greek-inspired pasta dish, if you like. Varieties include peppercorn, tomato-basil, and lemon, garlic, and oregano.

MAKES 4 servings **START TO FINISH** 25 minutes

8	ounces dried radiatore or rotini pasta (3 cups)
2	cups chopped plum tomatoes (4)
⅓	cup pitted kalamata olives, halved
¼	cup coarsely chopped red onion
¼	cup snipped fresh parsley
2	tablespoons olive oil or salad oil
¼	teaspoon salt
¼	teaspoon black pepper
1	cup crumbled feta cheese (4 ounces)
	Lemon wedges (optional)

① In a large saucepan cook pasta according to package directions.

② Meanwhile, in a large bowl combine tomatoes, olives, onion, parsley, oil, salt, and pepper. Drain pasta; toss with tomato mixture. Sprinkle with feta cheese. Serve warm with lemon wedges, if desired.

PER SERVING 384 cal, 15 g fat (5 g sat. fat), 25 mg chol, 594 mg sodium, 49 g carb, 3 g fiber, 12 g pro

Farfalle with Mushrooms and Spinach ♥

To thinly slice the spinach, stack several leaves, then roll into a bundle. Slice the bundle for pretty ribbons of spinach.

MAKES 2 servings **PREP** 10 minutes **COOK** 10 minutes

6	ounces packaged dried farfalle (bow tie pasta)
1	tablespoon olive oil
1	medium onion, chopped
1	cup sliced portobello or other fresh mushrooms
2	cloves garlic, minced
4	cups thinly sliced fresh spinach
1	teaspoon snipped fresh thyme
⅛	teaspoon black pepper
2	tablespoons shredded Parmesan cheese

① In a large saucepan cook farfalle according to package directions; drain.

② Meanwhile, in a large skillet heat oil over medium heat. Add onion, mushrooms, and garlic; cook and stir for 2 to 3 minutes or until mushrooms are nearly tender. Stir in spinach, thyme, and pepper; cook 1 minute or until heated through and spinach is slightly wilted. Stir in cooked pasta; toss gently to mix. Sprinkle with cheese.

PER SERVING 451 cal, 11 g fat (2 g sat. fat), 4 mg chol, 131 mg sodium, 74 g carb, 5 g fiber, 17 g pro

Farfalle with Mushrooms and Spinach

Ramen Noodles with Mushrooms and Shallots

Meaty mushrooms stand in for meat in this simple noodle dish flavored with shallots, soy sauce, and white wine.

MAKES 2 servings **START TO FINISH** 25 minutes

- 1   3-ounce package ramen noodles (any flavor)
- 6   ounces assorted fresh mushrooms, stemmed if necessary, and sliced
- ¼   cup finely chopped shallots (2 medium)
- 2   tablespoons butter or margarine
- ¼   cup dry white wine or reduced-sodium chicken broth
- 2   tablespoons soy sauce

① Cook noodles according to package directions. Reserve seasoning packet for another use. Drain and keep warm.

② Meanwhile, in a large skillet cook mushrooms and shallots in hot butter about 4 minutes or until tender. Remove from heat. Stir in wine and soy sauce. Return to heat. Cook, uncovered, about 5 minutes or until most of the liquid is evaporated. Add cooked noodles; toss to coat.

PER SERVING 375 cal, 22 g fat (8 g sat. fat), 31 mg chol, 1,010 mg sodium, 33 g carb, 1 g fiber, 10 g pro

Cheese Ravioli with Roasted Pepper Sauce

The only chopping this creamy tomato-sauced dish requires is a little prep for a green pepper. It virtually cooks itself!

MAKES 6 servings **START TO FINISH** 25 minutes

- 1   16-ounce package refrigerated 3-cheese ravioli or two 9-ounce packages refrigerated 4-cheese ravioli
- 1   25- to 32-ounce jar roasted red pepper marinara sauce
- 1   2.25-ounce can sliced pitted ripe olives, drained
- 1   4-ounce can mushroom stems and pieces, drained
- ½   cup finely chopped green sweet pepper
- ¾   cup whipping cream
- ¼   cup shredded fresh basil (optional)

① In a large saucepan cook ravioli according to package directions. Drain well.

② Meanwhile, for sauce in a medium saucepan combine marinara sauce, drained olives, drained mushrooms, green pepper, and whipping cream. Heat over medium heat until bubbly, stirring frequently. If desired, stir in basil. Divide ravioli among 6 plates. Pour sauce over ravioli; serve immediately.

PER SERVING 467 cal, 26 g fat (15 g sat. fat), 98 mg chol, 1,018 mg sodium, 44 g carb, 6 g fiber, 13 g pro

《 Noodles and pasta of all shapes and sizes—filled or not—make a quick and comforting supper. 》

Ramen Noodles with
Mushrooms and Shallots

Good and Healthy Macaroni and Cheese

Good and Healthy Macaroni and Cheese

This classic kid-favorite gets a healthful makeover in this all-in-one meal. A creamy low-fat cheese sauce coats multigrain pasta and the veggies of your choice.

MAKES 5 servings **START TO FINISH** 30 minutes

- 8 ounces dried multigrain elbow macaroni or penne pasta
- 1 cup chopped fresh or frozen mixed vegetables
- 1 12-ounce can evaporated fat-free milk
- 2 tablespoons all-purpose flour
- ¼ teaspoon salt
- ⅛ teaspoon black pepper
- 1¼ cups shredded reduced-fat cheddar cheese (5 ounces)
- 1 ounce American cheese, shredded
  Black pepper (optional)

① Cook pasta according to package directions, adding the vegetables the last 2 minutes of cooking. Drain; return to hot pan.

② Meanwhile, in a medium saucepan whisk together milk, flour, salt, and the ⅛ teaspoon pepper. Cook and stir over medium heat until thickened and bubbly. Add cheeses; cook and stir until melted.

③ Pour sauce over pasta and vegetables in pan. Heat through. If desired, sprinkle with additional pepper.

PER SERVING 344 cal, 9 g fat (5 g sat. fat), 28 mg chol, 553 mg sodium, 46 g carb, 4 g fiber, 23 g pro

quick tip Make this veggie-packed mac and cheese with one vegetable—or mix it up. To use fresh vegetables and still get a meal on the table in less than 30 minutes, look for bags of sliced carrots, cubed squash, or cut broccoli and cauliflower florets in the produce aisle of your supermarket.

Fettuccine Alfredo

Jazz up this favorite pasta dish with one of the variations below. It's company-worthy food in 30 minutes or less.

MAKES 4 servings **START TO FINISH** 30 minutes

- 8 ounces packaged dried fettuccine
- 2 cloves garlic, minced
- 2 tablespoons butter or margarine
- 1 cup whipping cream
- ½ teaspoon salt
- ⅛ teaspoon black pepper
- ½ cup grated Parmesan cheese
  Grated or finely shredded Parmesan cheese (optional)

① In a large saucepan cook fettuccine according to package directions; drain.

② Meanwhile, for sauce in a large saucepan cook garlic in hot butter over medium-high heat for 1 minute. Add cream, salt, and pepper. Bring to boiling; reduce heat. Boil gently, uncovered, for 3 minutes or until sauce begins to thicken. Remove from heat and stir in ½ cup Parmesan cheese. Drain pasta. Add pasta to hot sauce. Toss to combine. If desired, sprinkle each serving with additional cheese.

PER SERVING 514 cal, 32 g fat (19 g sat. fat), 107 mg chol, 511 mg sodium, 45 g carb, 2 g fiber, 13 g pro

Lemony Fettuccine Alfredo with Shrimp and Peas: Prepare as above, except add 8 ounces peeled, deveined uncooked shrimp and 1 cup frozen peas to pasta the last 1 minute of cooking. Stir 1 teaspoon finely shredded lemon peel and 1 tablespoon lemon juice into sauce before adding pasta.

Shiitake Fettuccine Alfredo: Prepare as above, except cook 1½ cups sliced shiitake or button mushrooms in the butter for 4 to 5 minutes or until tender before adding the cream, salt, and pepper.

Lemony Fettuccine Alfredo with Shrimp and Peas: Prepare as above, except add 8 ounces peeled, deveined uncooked shrimp and 1 cup frozen peas to pasta the last 1 minute of cooking. Stir 1 teaspoon finely shredded lemon peel and 1 tablespoon lemon juice into sauce before adding pasta.

Maybe soup can't always cure what ails you, but a warming bowl of soup or stew certainly cheers and comforts. With these quick-to-fix recipes, you can enjoy homemade soup more often with less effort.

157   161   170

SOUPS & STEWS

169

Cuban Black Bean Soup 🍲

Buy diced ham and you don't have to do a bit of chopping or prep work to make this hearty comforting soup.

MAKES 4 servings **START TO FINISH** 25 minutes

- 1 16-ounce jar mild or medium thick and chunky salsa or salsa with lime and garlic
- 1 14-ounce can chicken broth
- 1¾ cups water
- 1 15- to 16-ounce can black beans, rinsed and drained
- 8 ounces cooked ham, cubed
- 1 teaspoon ground cumin
- ½ cup sour cream
- ¼ cup salsa verde (optional)
  Crushed lime-flavor or regular tortilla chips (optional)

① In a large saucepan or Dutch oven combine salsa, broth, the water, beans, ham, and ground cumin. Bring to boiling; reduce heat. Simmer, covered, for 10 minutes.

② Top each serving with 2 tablespoons sour cream. If desired, top with salsa verde and crushed tortilla chips.

PER SERVING 175 cal, 6 g fat (3 g sat. fat), 12 mg chol, 1,359 mg sodium, 26 g carb, 8 g fiber, 10 g pro

Cuban Black Bean Soup with Peppers: Prepare as above, except substitute 2 cups frozen stir-fry vegetables (yellow, green, and red peppers, and onion) for the ham.

Cuban Black Bean Soup

Italian Spinach Soup

Watercress infuses this gorgeous green soup with a pleasantly peppery bite. The potato thickens the soup.

MAKES 6 servings **START TO FINISH** 30 minutes

- ½ cup chopped onion (1 medium)
- 4 cloves garlic, minced
- 2 teaspoons dried Italian seasoning, crushed
- 2 tablespoons butter
- 2 tablespoons dry sherry (optional)
- 2 14-ounce cans chicken broth
- 1 large potato, peeled and chopped
- 2 9-ounce packages fresh spinach or 1¼ pounds fresh spinach, washed and trimmed
- 2 cups watercress, tough stems removed
- 2 ounces Parmesan cheese, shaved
- 2 small tomatoes, quartered, seeded, and thinly sliced

① In a 4-quart Dutch oven cook onion, garlic, and Italian seasoning in hot butter over medium heat for 5 minutes or until onion is tender, stirring occasionally.

② If using sherry, remove Dutch oven from heat; slowly drizzle in sherry. Return to heat; cook and stir for 1 minute. Add broth and potato. Bring to boiling. Simmer, covered, for 10 minutes or until potato is tender. Remove from heat.

③ Set aside 2 cups of the spinach. Stir remaining spinach, half at a time, into soup just until wilted. Cook about 5 minutes.

④ Transfer soup, half at a time, to food processor or blender; cover and process or blend until smooth. Return to Dutch oven; heat through. Season with salt.

⑤ To serve, top with reserved spinach, watercress, Parmesan, and tomatoes.

PER SERVING 151 cal, 7 g fat (4 g sat. fat), 18 mg chol, 881 mg sodium, 16 g carb, 4 g fiber, 8 g pro

Indian Cauliflower Soup with
Garam Masala

Roasted Red Pepper Soup

Roasted Red Pepper Soup

Add a spoon of chive sour cream to give this beautiful red soup a bit of creamy goodness.

MAKES 4 servings **PREP** 15 minutes
COOK 15 minutes

- 1 cup chopped onion (1 large)
- 4 cloves garlic, minced
- 1 tablespoon olive oil
- 3 14-ounce cans vegetable or chicken broth (5¼ cups)
- 1 12-ounce jar roasted red sweet peppers, drained and sliced
- 1 cup peeled, chopped potato (1 medium)
- 1 teaspoon dried oregano, crushed, or 1 tablespoon snipped fresh oregano
- ½ teaspoon dried thyme, crushed, or 1 teaspoon snipped fresh thyme
- ¼ cup sour cream
- 1 tablespoon minced fresh chives

① In a large saucepan cook and stir onion and garlic in hot oil for 3 to 4 minutes or until tender. Stir in broth, red peppers, potato, oregano, and thyme. Bring to boiling; reduce heat. Simmer, covered, for 15 minutes. Cool slightly.

② Using a handheld immersion blender, blend until almost smooth; heat through. (Or place one-third at a time in a blender. Cover and blend until nearly smooth. Return all to saucepan; heat through.

③ In a small bowl combine sour cream and chives. To serve, ladle soup into bowls. Serve sour cream and chives on the side.

PER SERVING 137 cal, 6 g fat (2 g sat. fat), 5 mg chol, 1,181 mg sodium, 18 g carb, 3 g fiber, 2 g pro

Guacamole Soup

An avocado is perfectly ripe when it yields slightly to gentle pressure. Look for avocados with smooth, dark green skin and no blemishes or bruises.

MAKES 6 to 8 servings **START TO FINISH** 25 minutes

- 1 tablespoon vegetable oil
- 1 tablespoon butter
- 1 cup chopped red onion (1 large)
- 6 cloves garlic, minced
- 3 medium avocados, halved, seeded, peeled, and mashed (1¾ cups)
- 1 14-ounce can chicken broth or vegetable broth
- 1½ cups whipping cream
- 1 cup bottled salsa
- 2 tablespoons lime juice
- 2 tablespoons lemon juice
- 1 tablespoon ground cumin
  Assorted toppings: avocado slices, chopped red or yellow tomato, tortilla chips, lime slices, sour cream, and/or cooked shrimp (optional)

① In a 3-quart saucepan heat oil and butter over medium heat; add onion and garlic. Cook and stir about 5 minutes or until tender. Stir in avocados, broth, whipping cream, salsa, lime juice, lemon juice, and cumin; heat through. To serve, ladle soup into bowls. If desired, serve with assorted toppings.

PER SERVING 349 cal, 33 g fat (16 g sat. fat), 88 mg chol, 436 mg sodium, 13 g carb, 4 g fiber, 3 g pro

Guacamole Soup

Creamy Coconut-Lime Soup ♨

This is a quick take on that famous Thai soup, *tom kha kai*, a perfectly balanced bowl of sweet, sour, and spicy flavors.

MAKES 4 servings **START TO FINISH** 30 minutes

- 1 2- to 2½-pound purchased roasted chicken
- 2 cups water
- 1 14-ounce can unsweetened coconut milk
- 1½ cups thinly bias-sliced carrots (3 medium)
- ¼ cup lime juice
- 1 tablespoon soy sauce
- 2 teaspoons Thai seasoning
- ¼ teaspoon salt
   Thai seasoning (optional)
   Fresh cilantro sprigs (optional)
   Lime wedges (optional)

① Remove and discard skin and bones from chicken. Using two forks, pull chicken apart into shreds. In a large saucepan combine shredded chicken, the water, coconut milk, carrots, lime juice, soy sauce, 2 teaspoons Thai seasoning, and salt. Bring to boiling; reduce heat. Simmer, covered, about 8 minutes or until carrots are crisp-tender.

② Ladle soup into bowls. If desired, top with additional Thai seasoning and cilantro; serve with lime wedges.

PER SERVING 487 cal, 38 g fat (24 g sat. fat), 125 mg chol, 1,437 mg sodium, 11 g carb, 1 g fiber, 29 g pro

Creamy Coconut-Lime Soup

Make-It-Mine Soup ♨

Customize this hearty soup with your choice of meat, vegetables, and beans.

MAKES 4 servings **START TO FINISH** 30 minutes

- 2 tablespoons vegetable oil
- 8 ounces boneless chicken, turkey, beef steak, or lean pork, cut into 1-inch pieces
- 3 cups assorted chopped vegetables, such as onions, carrots, potatoes, zucchini, sweet peppers, tomatoes, small broccoli florets, green peas, and/or corn
- 1 32-ounce carton beef broth or chicken broth
- ½ of a 6-ounce can tomato paste (⅓ cup)
- 1 ounce envelope onion soup mix
- ½ teaspoon dried rosemary, oregano, basil, or Italian seasoning
- 1 cup canned beans, such as kidney, black, great Northern, or navy, rinsed and drained, or cooked rice or pasta
   Salt
   Black pepper

① In a 4- to 5-quart Dutch oven heat 1 tablespoon of the oil over medium-high heat. Add meat; cook and stir until meat is brown and cooked through. If necessary, drain off fat. Remove meat from pan; set aside.

② In the same Dutch oven heat the remaining 1 tablespoon oil over medium-high heat. Add vegetables; cook and stir for 3 to 5 minutes or until vegetables are crisp-tender. Return meat to Dutch oven.

③ Stir in broth, tomato paste, onion soup mix, and dried herb. Bring to boiling over high heat; reduce heat. Simmer, covered, for 15 minutes. Stir in beans. Season to taste with salt and black pepper.

PER SERVING 249 cal, 10 g fat (1 g sat. fat), 40 mg chol, 1,825 mg sodium, 22 g carb, 2 g fiber, 18 g pro

California Cioppino

California Cioppino 🍲 ♥

Fresh fennel has an anise/licoricelike flavor. Add crushed anise seeds if you really like that taste, crushing the seeds with a mortar and pestle.

MAKES 8 servings **START TO FINISH** 35 minutes

- 2 pounds fresh skinless salmon or cod fillets, and/or sea scallops
- 2 fennel bulbs, trimmed and thinly sliced
- 3 tablespoons olive oil
- 4 cloves garlic, minced
- 3 cups coarsely chopped tomatoes (3 large)
- 1 14- to 15-ounce can fish stock or chicken broth
- 1 teaspoon dried oregano, crushed, or 2 teaspoons snipped fresh oregano
- ½ teaspoon anise seeds, crushed (optional)
  Salt
  Black pepper
  Fennel leaves or shredded fresh basil

① Rinse fish and/or scallops; pat dry with paper towels. If using fish, cut into 2-inch pieces. Set aside.

② In a 4- to 6-quart Dutch oven cook sliced fennel in hot oil over medium heat about 10 minutes or until tender. Add garlic; cook and stir for 1 minute.

③ Add tomatoes, stock, dried oregano (if using), and, if desired, anise seeds; bring to boiling. Stir in fish and/or scallops. Return to boiling; reduce heat. Simmer, uncovered, for 6 to 8 minutes or until fish flakes easily when tested with a fork and/or scallops are opaque. Season to taste with salt and pepper. Stir in fresh oregano (if using). Garnish each serving with fennel leaves.

PER SERVING 178 cal, 6 g fat (1 g sat. fat), 49 mg chol, 169 mg sodium, 9 g carb, 3 g fiber, 22 g pro

quick tip   To make fish stock, use 1½ pounds fresh or frozen fish heads and tails or drawn lean fish (such as cod, pike, flounder, or haddock). Thaw fish, if frozen. Rinse fish; pat dry with paper towels. Place fish in a Dutch oven. Add 4 cups water; 1 stalk celery with leaves, cut up; half of medium onion, cut into wedges; 2 tablespoons lemon juice; 2 teaspoons dried marjoram, crushed; 2 teaspoons grated fresh ginger or ½ teaspoon ground ginger; 2 cloves garlic, halved; ¼ teaspoon salt; and ¼ teaspoon dry mustard. Bring to boiling; reduce heat. Simmer, covered, for 45 minutes. Strain stock; discard solids. Makes 3½ cups.

Shrimp and Soba Pot

Soba noodles, made with buckwheat flour, have a wonderfully nutty flavor and pretty purple-brown hue.

MAKES 6 servings **START TO FINISH** 35 minutes

- 12 ounces fresh or frozen medium shrimp in shells
- 1 32-ounce carton reduced-sodium chicken broth or vegetable broth
- 6 ounces dried soba (buckwheat noodles)
- 4 cups sliced fresh shiitake mushrooms
- 6 green onions, cut into 1-inch pieces
- 1 tablespoon grated fresh ginger
- 4 cloves garlic, minced
- 2 teaspoons peanut oil or vegetable oil
- 1 bunch bok choy, trimmed and coarsely chopped
- 1 sweet potato, peeled and cubed
- 1 8-ounce can sliced water chestnuts, rinsed and drained
- 1 teaspoon toasted sesame oil (optional)
  Lime wedges
  Asian chili sauce (optional)
  Small sprigs fresh cilantro (optional)
  Toasted sesame seeds (optional)

① Thaw shrimp, if frozen. Peel and devein shrimp, reserving shells. Rinse shrimp; pat dry with paper towels. Coarsely chop shrimp; cover and chill until needed. Rinse shrimp shells in a colander; drain.

② In a large saucepan combine shrimp shells and broth. Bring to boiling; reduce heat. Simmer, uncovered, for 5 minutes. Strain broth into a bowl; discard shells. Rinse out saucepan. In the saucepan cook soba according to package directions; drain. Return to hot pan; cover and keep warm.

③ Meanwhile, in a Dutch oven cook mushrooms, green onions, ginger, and garlic in hot peanut oil over medium heat about 5 minutes or until mushrooms are tender. Stir in strained broth, bok choy, sweet potato, and water chestnuts. Bring to boiling; reduce heat. Simmer, uncovered, about 6 minutes or until bok choy and sweet potato are tender. Stir in shrimp and, if desired, sesame oil. Cook about 1 minute more or until shrimp are opaque.

④ Serve soup in bowls over soba. Serve with lime wedges and, if desired, chili sauce, cilantro, and sesame seeds.

PER SERVING 244 cal, 3 g fat (1 g sat. fat), 86 mg chol, 717 mg sodium, 38 g carb, 4 g fiber, 20 g pro

Easy Maryland Crab Bisque

Serve this creamy bisque (or the shrimp variation) with watercress salad and crusty rolls.

START TO FINISH 20 minutes

2¾	cups milk
1	10.75-ounce can condensed cream of asparagus soup
1	10.75-ounce can condensed cream of mushroom soup
1	cup half-and-half or light cream
1	5- to 6-ounce can crabmeat, drained, flaked, and cartilage removed
3	tablespoons dry sherry or milk
	Fresh chives (optional)

① In a 3-quart saucepan combine milk, asparagus soup, mushroom soup, and half-and-half. Bring just to boiling over medium heat, stirring frequently. Stir in crabmeat and dry sherry; heat through. To serve, ladle bisque into bowls. If desired, garnish each serving with chives.

PER SERVING 225 cal, 12 g fat (5 g sat. fat), 51 mg chol, 882 mg sodium, 15 g carb, 0 g fiber, 12 g pro

Easy Shrimp Bisque: Prepare as directed, except substitute cream of shrimp soup for the cream of mushroom soup and 8 ounces peeled and deveined cooked small shrimp for the crabmeat.

Cheesy Corn and Potato Chowder

Add the cheese in small handfuls and let each one melt before adding the next so the cheese melts smoothly and doesn't clump.

MAKES 6 servings **START TO FINISH** 30 minutes

4	cups vegetable broth
½	of a 32-ounce package frozen diced hash brown potatoes (3½ cups)
2	cups frozen whole kernel corn
1	chopped cup onion (1 large)
½	cup chopped celery (1 stalk)
1½	cups milk
3	tablespoons all-purpose flour
¼	teaspoon salt
¼	teaspoon black pepper
1	8-ounce package shredded cheddar cheese

① In a 4-quart Dutch oven combine vegetable broth, hash browns, corn, onion, and celery. Bring to boiling; reduce heat. Simmer, covered, for 12 to 15 minutes or until potatoes are tender, stirring occasionally.

② Meanwhile, in a 2-cup glass measure whisk together milk, flour, salt, and pepper. Add to vegetables. Cook and stir over medium heat until thick and bubbly. Gradually stir in cheese until melted.

PER SERVING 432 cal, 23 g fat (12 g sat. fat), 45 mg chol, 1,019 mg sodium, 44 g carb, 4 g fiber, 16 g pro

 Creamy bisques and chowders are especially loved in New England, where they warm the body during the region's cold rainy autumns.

Smoky Chile and Corn Chowder

Smoky Chile and Corn Chowder ♥

The smokiness of this delicious chicken and corn chowder comes from chipotle pepper—in the soup itself—and a red pepper puree garnish infused with smoked paprika.

MAKES 4 servings **START TO FINISH** 35 minutes

- 1 recipe Roasted Red Pepper Puree
- ⅓ cup chopped onion (1 small)
- 1 tablespoon chopped canned chipotle pepper in adobo sauce
- 1 teaspoon butter
- 4 cups fresh corn kernels or frozen whole kernel corn
- 1 14.5-ounce can reduced-sodium chicken broth
- 8 ounces skinless, boneless chicken breast halves or pork tenderloin, cut into bite-size pieces
- 1 12-ounce can evaporated nonfat milk or low-fat milk
- 3 tablespoons snipped fresh cilantro
- 2 tablespoons crumbled queso fresco or ¼ cup shredded Monterey Jack cheese (1 ounce) (optional)

① Prepare Roasted Red Pepper Puree. In a large saucepan cook onion and chipotle pepper in ½ teaspoon of the butter over medium heat about 5 minutes or until onion is tender. Stir in 1½ cups of the corn and the broth; cook for 3 minutes. Cool slightly.

② Transfer corn mixture to a blender or food processor. Cover and blend or process until nearly smooth; set aside.

③ In the same saucepan cook chicken in the remaining ½ teaspoon butter over medium-high heat until brown. Stir in pureed corn, the remaining 2½ cups corn kernels, and evaporated milk. Cook and stir until heated through. Stir in cilantro.

④ Ladle soup into bowls. Drizzle with Roasted Red Pepper Puree and sprinkle with cheese, if desired.

Roasted Red Pepper Puree: In a blender or food processor combine one 7-ounce jar (1 cup) roasted red sweet peppers, drained, and, if desired, ½ teaspoon smoked paprika. Cover and blend or process until smooth. Refrigerate any leftover puree up to 1 week. Makes about ¾ cup.

PER SERVING 306 cal, 3 g fat (1 g sat. fat), 39 mg chol, 411 mg sodium, 48 g carb, 5 g fiber, 26 g pro

Spring Chicken Stew 🍲

Baby carrots with feathery green tops have better texture and sweeter flavor than those without.

MAKES 4 servings **START TO FINISH** 30 minutes

- 1 lemon
- 1¼ pounds skinless, boneless chicken thighs
  Salt
  Black pepper
- 1 tablespoon olive oil
- 8 ounces baby carrots with tops, trimmed and halved lengthwise
- 1 12-ounce jar chicken gravy
- 1½ cups water
- 1 tablespoon Dijon mustard
- 2 heads baby bok choy, quartered
  Snipped fresh lemon thyme (optional)

① Finely shred peel from lemon; set peel aside. Juice lemon and set juice aside. Season chicken lightly with salt and pepper.

② In a Dutch oven heat oil over medium-high heat; add chicken. Cook for 2 to 3 minutes or until chicken is brown, turning occasionally.

③ Add carrots, gravy, and the water to chicken in Dutch oven. Stir in mustard. Bring to boiling. Place bok choy on top. Reduce heat. Cover and simmer about 10 minutes or just until chicken is no longer pink (180°F) and vegetables are tender. Add lemon juice to taste.

④ Ladle into bowls. Top with lemon peel and lemon thyme.

PER SERVING 273 cal, 12 g fat (2 g sat. fat), 117 mg chol, 909 mg sodium, 13 g carb, 3 g fiber, 31 g pro

Moroccan Chicken Stew

In addition to the aromatic combination of spices, the sweet-salty blend of raisins and olives gives this stew exotic Moroccan flavor.

MAKES 6 servings   **START TO FINISH** 35 minutes

- 1   tablespoon all-purpose flour
- 1   teaspoon ground coriander
- 1   teaspoon ground cumin
- 1   teaspoon ground paprika
- ½   teaspoon salt
- ½   teaspoon ground cinnamon
- 1   pound skinless, boneless chicken thighs, cut into 1-inch pieces
- 2   medium onions, cut into wedges
- 3   cloves garlic, minced
- 1   tablespoon olive oil
- 1   28-ounce can crushed tomatoes, undrained
- 1   15-ounce can garbanzo beans (chickpeas), rinsed and drained
- 1½ cups water
- ½   cup raisins
- ⅓   cup small pitted ripe olives
- 3   cups hot cooked couscous
- ¼   cup snipped fresh cilantro

① In a shallow bowl combine flour, coriander, cumin, paprika, salt, and cinnamon. Coat chicken with the flour mixture; set aside.

② In a 4-quart Dutch oven cook onions and garlic in hot oil over medium heat for 4 to 6 minutes or until tender. Remove from Dutch oven, reserving oil in pan. Add chicken to pan, half at a time. Cook quickly until lightly browned, stirring frequently. Return all chicken and onions to pan. Add tomatoes, garbanzo beans, the water, raisins, and olives. Bring to boiling; reduce heat. Cover and simmer about 10 minutes or until chicken is tender, stirring occasionally. Serve over couscous. Sprinkle with cilantro.

PER SERVING 394 cal, 7 g fat (1 g sat. fat), 60 mg chol, 858 mg sodium, 57 g carb, 8 g fiber, 24 g pro

Spiced Meatball Stew

Serve this hearty meal-in-a-bowl with crusty Italian bread or thick chunks of focaccia.

MAKES 8 servings   **START TO FINISH** 30 minutes

- 1   16-ounce package frozen cooked Italian-style meatballs (32 meatballs)
- 3   cups green beans cut into 1-inch pieces or frozen cut green beans
- 2   cups sliced carrots (4 medium)
- 1   14.5-ounce can beef broth
- 2   teaspoons Worcestershire sauce
- ½   to ¾ teaspoon ground allspice
- ½   teaspoon ground cinnamon
- 2   14.5-ounce cans diced tomatoes, undrained

① In a Dutch oven combine meatballs, beans, carrots, broth, Worcestershire sauce, allspice, and cinnamon. Bring to boiling; reduce heat. Simmer, covered, for 10 minutes.

② Stir in tomatoes. Return to boiling; reduce heat. Simmer, covered, about 5 minutes more or until vegetables are crisp-tender.

PER SERVING 230 cal, 15 g fat (7 g sat. fat), 44 mg chol, 976 mg sodium, 14 g carb, 4 g fiber, 10 g pro

Spiced Meatball Stew

It's no wonder that many cooks say that grilling is their favorite way to cook. Hot coals bring out so much flavor in food that few extra ingredients are needed. These tasty recipes will wow your friends and family.

177

190

201

FROM THE GRILL

206

Basil-Mozzarella Cheeseburgers 🍔

Meat patties tend to shrink when cooked, forming a domed shape that can make it hard to keep the toppings from sliding off. To avoid this, make a slight indentation in the center of each patty before cooking. After it's cooked, it should be nice and flat—a perfect platform for toppings.

MAKES 4 servings   **PREP** 15 minutes   **GRILL** 14 minutes

- ¼ **cup finely chopped onion**
- 2 **tablespoons fine dry bread crumbs**
- 2 **tablespoons finely chopped green sweet pepper (optional)**
- 2 **tablespoons ketchup**
- 1 **tablespoon prepared horseradish**
- 1 **tablespoon yellow mustard**
- ½ **teaspoon salt**
- ¼ **teaspoon black pepper**
- 1 **pound lean ground beef**
- 4 **slices smoked or regular mozzarella cheese**
- 4 **whole wheat hamburger buns, split and toasted**
  Fresh basil leaves
- ¼ **cup Red Sweet Pepper Relish**

① In a medium bowl combine onion, bread crumbs, sweet pepper (if desired), ketchup, horseradish, mustard, salt, and black pepper. Add ground beef; mix well. Shape meat mixture into four ¾-inch-thick patties.

② Place patties on rack of uncovered grill directly over medium coals. Grill for 14 to 18 minutes or until done (160°F), turning once halfway through grilling and topping with cheese during last 2 minutes of grilling. (For a gas grill, preheat grill. Reduce heat to medium. Place patties on grill rack over heat. Cover and grill as above.)

③ Serve patties on toasted buns with basil leaves and Red Sweet Pepper Relish.

Red Sweet Pepper Relish: In a small bowl combine ½ cup finely chopped roasted red sweet pepper; 2 teaspoons snipped fresh thyme or ½ teaspoon dried thyme, crushed; 2 teaspoons olive oil; and ¼ teaspoon ground black pepper. Cover and chill until ready to serve.

PER SERVING 422 cal, 20 g fat (8 g sat. fat), 89 mg chol, 930 mg sodium, 27 g carb, 3 g fiber, 32 g pro

Blue Cheese-Stuffed Burger with Red Onion and Spinach 🍔

Make sure the two halves of each patty are well sealed so all of that yummy blue cheese doesn't melt and leak out during cooking!

MAKES 4 servings   **PREP** 15 minutes   **GRILL** 14 minutes

- 1 **pound ground beef**
- 1 **tablespoon Worcestershire sauce**
- 1 **teaspoon freshly ground black pepper**
- ⅓ **to ½ cup crumbled blue cheese (about 2 ounces)**
- 1 **medium red onion**
  Olive oil
- 4 **hamburger buns, split**
- 1 **cup fresh baby spinach**

① In a medium bowl combine beef, Worcestershire sauce, and black pepper. On waxed paper, shape into 8 thin 4-inch-diameter patties. Place 1 tablespoon of the blue cheese in center of 4 of the patties. Top with remaining 4 patties; pinch edges to seal.

② Brush onion slices with olive oil; sprinkle with salt.

③ Place burgers and onions directly over medium-high heat. Grill for 14 to 18 minutes or until done (160°F), turning once halfway through grilling. Drizzle cut slides of buns with olive oil. Grill, cut sides down, the last 1 minute of grilling. (For a gas grill, preheat grill. Reduce heat to medium. Place patties on grill rack over heat. Cover and grill as above.)

④ Serve burgers on buns with grilled onions, spinach, and remaining cheese.

PER SERVING 497 cal, 31 g fat (12 g sat. fat), 89 mg chol, 638 mg sodium, 26 g carb, 2 g fiber, 27 g pro

quick tip When forming patties or meatballs with ground meat, keep the mixture from sticking to your hands by dipping your hands in a bowl of cool water before working with the meat. Dip as often as needed to prevent sticking.

Blue Cheese-Stuffed Burger with
Red Onion and Spinach

Great Grilled Burgers

Great Grilled Burgers

The definition of lean ground beef, according to the USDA, specifies that it must not contain any more than 10 percent fat. Extra-lean ground beef can't contain any more than 5 percent fat.

MAKES 2 servings **PREP** 15 minutes **GRILL** 14 minutes

- 1½ pounds lean ground beef
- 1 teaspoon dried Italian seasoning, crushed
- ½ teaspoon salt
- ½ teaspoon black pepper
- ½ cup finely chopped onion
- 4 slices cheddar, Edam, or Monterey Jack cheese (4 ounces)
- 4 hamburger buns, split and toasted
  Toppings, such as lettuce leaves, tomato slices, onion slices, and/or bread and butter pickles
  Ketchup and/or yellow mustard

① In a large bowl combine beef, Italian seasoning, salt, and pepper until well mixed. Add finely chopped onion to the remaining beef mixture in the bowl; mix well. Lightly shape into four ¾-inch-thick patties.

② For a charcoal grill, grill patties on the rack of an uncovered grill directly over medium coals for 14 to 18 minutes or until done (160°F), turning once halfway through grilling. Top each pattie with a slice of cheese. Grill about 1 minute more or until cheese is just melted. (For a gas grill, preheat grill. Reduce heat to medium. Place patties on grill rack over heat. Cover and grill as above.) To serve, fill buns with grilled patties and toppings. Serve with ketchup and/or mustard.

PER SERVING 540 cal, 25 g fat (11 g sat. fat), 131 mg chol, 945 mg sodium, 31 g carb, 2 g fiber, 44 g pro

Meatball and Vegetable Kabobs

Kids will love this meatball-based meal-on-a-stick.

MAKES 4 servings **PREP** 20 minutes **GRILL** 8 minutes

- ½ of a 6-ounce can tomato paste with Italian seasonings (⅓ cup)
- ¼ cup water
- ½ teaspoon Italian seasoning, crushed
- 16 1-inch refrigerated or frozen Italian-style meatballs, thawed
- 2 small zucchini
- 8 large cherry tomatoes
- 8 metal or bamboo skewers (see quick tip)
  Nonstick cooking spray

① Preheat indoor electric grill or broiler. In a medium bowl combine tomato paste, the water, and Italian seasoning to make a thick sauce. Add meatballs to sauce, stir to coat; set aside.

② Using a vegetable peeler, cut 4 evenly spaced strips from zucchini. Cut zucchini in 1-inch cubes.

③ On skewers, alternately thread meatballs and zucchini; thread a tomato on each end. Lightly coat kabobs with nonstick cooking spray. For a charcoal grill, grill kabobs 8 to 10 minutes or until done, turning once halfway through grilling. Brush remaining sauce on kabobs during last 2 minutes of cooking. (For a gas grill, preheat grill. Reduce heat to medium. Place kabobs on grill rack over heat. Cover and grill as above.)

PER SERVING 222 cal, 15 g fat (7 g sat. fat), 43 mg chol, 623 mg sodium, 12 g carb, 3 g fiber, 10 g pro

quick tip Soak bamboo skewers in water 30 minutes before using to prevent the skewers from burning.

Grilled Texas Steak Sandwiches with Dilled Horseradish Sauce

This steak knife-and-fork open-faced sandwich will satisfy even the heartiest appetites.

MAKES 4 servings **START TO FINISH** 20 minutes

- 2 10-ounce top round steaks
- Olive oil
- Salt and black pepper
- ¼ cup sour cream
- 2 to 3 tablespoons horseradish mustard
- 1 tablespoon snipped fresh dill
- 4 thick slices of bread
- Fresh dill sprigs (optional)

① Trim any fat from steaks; halve steaks crosswise. Lightly brush steaks with oil and sprinkle with salt and pepper. For a charcoal grill, grill directly over medium for 10 to 12 minutes for medium-rare (145°F) or 12 to 15 minutes for medium (160°F) turning once halfway through grilling. (For a gas grill, preheat grill. Reduce heat to medium. Place steaks on grill rack over heat. Cover and grill as above.)

② Meanwhile, for horseradish sauce, in a small bowl combine sour cream, horseradish mustard, and dill.

③ Remove steaks to platter. Lightly brush each side of the bread with olive oil. Grill bread 1 minute per side. Serve steaks on grilled toast with horseradish sauce. If desired, top with dill and additional salt and pepper.

PER SERVING 434 cal, 25 g fat (8 g sat. fat), 71 mg chol, 485 mg sodium, 21 g carb, 1 g fiber, 33 g pro

Grilled Texas Steak Sandwiches with Dilled Horseradish Sauce

Grilled Steak and Peppers 🍲 ♥

Thick, reddish-brown and spicy-sweet hoisin sauce—made with soybeans, garlic, vinegar, salt, sugar, and chile peppers—is a terrific shortcut to great flavor.

MAKES 4 servings **PREP** 15 minutes **GRILL** 12 minutes

- 3 medium yellow and/or red sweet peppers, cut into 1-inch-thick wedges
- 1 medium red onion, cut into 1-inch-wide wedges
- 3 tablespoons bottled hoisin sauce
- 2 tablespoons dry red wine
- 1 tablespoon olive oil
- 4 4-ounce beef tenderloin steaks, cut 1 inch thick
- ¼ teaspoon salt
- ¼ teaspoon coarsely ground black pepper

① In a medium bowl toss together sweet peppers, red onion, hoisin sauce, red wine, and olive oil. Thread vegetables onto four 10-inch wood or metal skewers (see quick tip, page 177); set aside.

② Trim fat from steaks. Sprinkle both sides of each steak with salt and pepper; rub in with your fingers. For a charcoal grill, place steaks and kabobs on the rack of an uncovered grill directly over medium coals for 10 to 12 minutes for medium-rare (145°F) or 12 to 15 minutes for medium (160°F), turning once halfway through grilling. Grill kabobs about 12 minutes or until vegetables are crisp-tender and lightly charred, turning once halfway through grilling. (For a gas grill, preheat grill. Reduce heat to medium. Place steaks and kabobs on grill rack over heat. Cover and grill as above.)

PER SERVING 284 cal, 11 g fat (3 g sat. fat), 76 mg chol, 407 mg sodium, 17 g carb, 2 g fiber, 27 g pro

Grilled Steak Bruschetta Salad

Grilled Pork and Pineapple

Grilled Pork and Pineapple ♥

For the whole rings of cored pineapple in this recipe, buy a prepared fresh pineapple from the produce section of the grocery store.

MAKES 4 servings **PREP** 20 minutes **GRILL** 8 minutes

- 4 boneless top loin pork chops cut ¾ inch thick (about 1¼ pounds total)
- ¼ teaspoon salt
- ¼ teaspoon black pepper
- 1 peeled and cored fresh pineapple
- 1 6-ounce carton nonfat plain yogurt
- ⅓ cup low-sugar orange marmalade
- 2 tablespoons coarsely chopped toasted pecans (see quick tip, page 76)
- 1 tablespoon snipped fresh thyme or 1 teaspoon dried thyme

① Sprinkle both sides of pork with salt and pepper. Cut pineapple crosswise into ½-inch-thick slices; set aside. Combine yogurt and 2 tablespoons of the marmalade; set aside.

② For a charcoal grill, grill chops on the rack of an uncovered grill directly over medium coals for 3 minutes. Turn chops; add pineapple to grill. Brush chops and pineapple with remaining marmalade. Grill 3 to 5 minutes more or until pork is slightly pink in the center (145°F) and pineapple has light grill marks, turning pineapple once.

③ Arrange pineapple and chops on serving plates. Spoon yogurt mixture on chops and pineapple; sprinkle with nuts and fresh thyme.

PER SERVING 295 cal, 5 g fat (2 g sat. fat), 94 mg chol, 242 mg sodium, 28 g carb, 2 g fiber, 35 g pro

---

quick tip If you don't need a fresh pineapple to be cut into rings, you can buy a whole fresh pineapple; breaking one down is really quite easy. First twist the crown off, then trim a piece off of each end of the fruit. To remove the scaly skin, cut down the fruit, from top to bottom, all of the way around it. Cut the peeled fruit in quarters—you'll be able to see the core in each piece. Cut under the core with a long sharp knife to remove it.

Italian Pork Chops on a Stick

Don't wait until State Fair time to enjoy this meaty treat. This version is infused with the flavors of rosemary, oregano, garlic, basil, and fennel.

MAKES 4 servings **PREP** 20 minutes
MARINATE 4 hours **GRILL** 7 minutes

- 2 tablespoons olive oil
- 1 tablespoon red wine vinegar
- 2 teaspoons snipped fresh rosemary
- 2 teaspoons snipped fresh oregano
- 3 cloves garlic, minced
- 1 teaspoon fennel seeds, crushed
- 1 teaspoon dried basil, crushed
- ½ teaspoon dry mustard
- ½ teaspoon salt
- ¼ teaspoon black pepper
- 4 5- to 6-ounce boneless pork top loin chops, cut ¾ inch thick

① For marinade, in a small bowl combine oil, vinegar, snipped rosemary, oregano, garlic, fennel seeds, basil, dry mustard, salt, and pepper.

② Butterfly each pork chop by cutting horizontally to, but not through, the other side. Lay open the chops. Brush both sides of each chop with marinade. Place chops in a resealable plastic bag set in a shallow dish. Seal bag. Marinate in the refrigerator for 4 to 24 hours.

③ Remove chops from bag. Thread chops, accordion-style, onto four 10- to 12-inch wood or metal skewers (see quick tip, page 177), leaving enough room to hold one end of each skewer. (For additional stability, thread each chop onto 2 skewers.)

④ For a charcoal grill, place chops on the rack of an uncovered grill directly over medium coals. Grill for 6 to 8 minutes or until pork is slightly pink in the center (145°F), turning once halfway through grilling. (For a gas grill, preheat grill. Reduce heat to medium. Place chops on grill rack over heat. Cover and grill as above.)

PER SERVING 288 cal, 17 g fat (4 g sat. fat), 95 mg chol, 360 mg sodium, 1 g carb, 0 g fiber, 31 g pro

Grilled Pork Chops with Chile Rub and Chutney

To section an orange, trim a slice off each end of the fruit. Cut the fruit from top to bottom to remove the peel and white pith. With a small, thin, sharp knife, cut on either side of each orange section to release it from the membrane. (Hold the fruit over a bowl to catch juices).

MAKES 4 servings **PREP** 30 minutes

- 1   medium sweet onion, thinly sliced
- ½   teaspoon cumin seeds
- ¼   teaspoon sea salt
- 1   tablespoon olive oil
- 4   bone-in pork loin chops, ¾ inch thick (about 2 pounds total)
- 1   large chipotle pepper in adobo sauce, finely chopped (see quick tip, page 47)
- 2   oranges, peeled, seeded, and sectioned
- ¼   cup orange juice

① In a large skillet cook onion slices, cumin seeds, and sea salt in hot oil over medium heat for 12 to 15 minutes or until onion is tender and golden brown, stirring occasionally.

② Meanwhile, trim fat from pork chops. Rub chopped chipotle pepper onto chops. For a charcoal grill, grill chops on the rack of an uncovered grill directly over medium coals for 6 to 8 minutes or until pork is slightly pink in the center (145°F), turning once halfway through grilling. (For a gas grill, preheat grill; reduce heat to medium. Place chops on grill rack over heat. Cover and grill as above.)

③ Add orange sections and orange juice to onion mixture. Heat to boiling; reduce heat. Simmer, uncovered, for 5 minutes, stirring occasionally. Serve over grilled pork chops.

PER SERVING 289 cal, 14 g fat (4 g sat. fat), 78 mg chol, 207 mg sodium, 16 g carb, 3 g fiber, 25 g pro

Grilled Pork and Peach Salad ♥

Hold off on making this salad until the peak of peach season—late July and August in most parts of the country—for the sweetest, juiciest, most flavorful peaches.

MAKES 4 servings **PREP** 20 minutes **GRILL** 10 minutes

- 1   1-pound pork tenderloin
- 2   medium peaches or nectarines
- 2   tablespoons honey
- 2   tablespoons orange juice
- 1   tablespoon low-sodium soy sauce
- ½   teaspoon curry powder
- ¼   teaspoon black pepper
- 3   cups torn Bibb lettuce
- 3   cups packaged fresh baby spinach
- ¼   cup green onions, bias sliced (2)

① Trim pork and cut into 1-inch cubes. Pit peaches and cut into 1-inch cubes. On four 10-inch wood or metal skewers (see quick tip, page 177), thread pork cubes. On three more 10-inch wood or metal skewers, thread peach cubes.

② For a charcoal grill, grill kabobs on the grill rack directly over medium coals for 6 to 8 minutes for pork or until slightly pink in the center (145°F), turning once halfway through grilling. For peaches grill 8 to 10 minutes or until peaches are browned. (For a gas grill, preheat grill. Reduce heat to medium. Place skewers on grill rack over heat. Cover and grill as above.)

③ Meanwhile, in a large bowl stir together honey, orange juice, soy sauce, curry powder, and pepper. When pork kabobs are done, remove pork and peaches from skewers and place in honey mixture; toss to coat.

④ To serve, arrange lettuce and spinach on 4 serving plates. Spoon pork and peaches on greens. Sprinkle with green onions.

PER SERVING 207 cal, 3 g fat (1 g sat. fat), 54 mg chol, 444 mg sodium, 20 g carb, 3 g fiber, 26 g pro

Provençal Grilled Chicken and Herbed Penne

Five-Spice Pork Kabobs ♥

Serve each person two kabobs for a main dish—or just one kabob as an appetizer.

MAKES 4 servings **PREP** 20 minutes **GRILL** 6 minutes

 2 tablespoons ketchup
 1 tablespoon soy sauce
 2 teaspoons packed brown sugar
 1 teaspoon Chinese five-spice powder
 1½ pounds pork tenderloin
 8 bamboo or metal skewers
 ¼ cup peanuts
 ¼ cup cilantro sprigs
    Lime wedges (optional)

① For sauce, in a small bowl combine ketchup, soy sauce, brown sugar, and five-spice powder.

② Trim the tenderloin; thinly slice. Thread slices onto 8 bamboo or metal skewers (see quick tip, page 177). Brush skewered meat with some of the sauce.

③ For a charcoal grill, grill kabobs on the grill rack directly over medium coals for 6 to 8 minutes or until slightly pink in the center (145°F), turning once halfway through grilling and brushing with remaining sauce. (For a gas grill, preheat grill. Reduce heat to medium. Place kabobs on grill rack over heat. Cover and grill as above.) To serve, sprinkle with peanuts and cilantro. Serve with lime wedges, if desired.

PER SERVING 280 cal, 11 g fat (3 g sat. fat), 111 mg chol, 458 mg sodium, 7 g carb, 1 g fiber, 38 g pro

Provençal Grilled Chicken and Herbed Penne

Fines herbes is a classic quartet of herbs commonly used in French cooking. The traditional combination is chervil, chives, parsley, and tarragon.

MAKES 4 servings **START TO FINISH** 25 minutes

 8 ounces dried tomato or garlic and herb-flavor penne pasta or plain penne pasta
 4 medium skinless, boneless chicken breast halves (about 1 pound total)
 1 medium zucchini, halved lengthwise
 8 thick asparagus spears, trimmed (8 to 10 ounces total)
 3 tablespoons olive oil
 1 tablespoon fines herbes or herbes de Provence, crushed
 ½ teaspoon salt
 1 tablespoon snipped fresh thyme
 ½ cup finely shredded Asiago or Pecorino Romano cheese

① Cook pasta according to package directions. Meanwhile, rinse chicken; pat dry. Brush chicken, zucchini, and asparagus with 1 tablespoon of the oil; sprinkle all sides with fines herbes and salt.

② For a charcoal grill, place chicken in the center of a lightly greased rack of an uncovered grill. Place the zucchini and asparagus around chicken. Grill directly over medium heat for 12 to 15 minutes or until chicken is tender and no longer pink (170°F) and vegetables are tender, turning once halfway through grilling. (For a gas grill, preheat grill. Reduce heat to medium. Place chicken on grill rack over heat. Cover and grill as above.)

③ Transfer chicken and vegetables to cutting board; cool slightly. Cut chicken and zucchini into 1-inch cubes; slice asparagus into 1-inch lengths pieces. Drain pasta; return to saucepan. Add chicken, vegetables, remaining oil, and thyme to pasta; toss well. Divide among 4 dinner plates; top with cheese and season with pepper.

PER SERVING 480 cal, 17 g fat (2 g sat. fat), 69 mg chol, 492 mg sodium, 45 g carb, 4 g fiber, 35 g pro

Chicken with Two-Peach Salsa ♥

Bottled salsa gets a flavor boost from fresh peaches plucked at the peak of the season.

MAKES 4 servings **PREP** 10 minutes **GRILL** 12 minutes

- ½ **cup chunky salsa**
- 1 **yellow peach, finely chopped**
- 1 **white peach, finely chopped**
- 2 **tablespoons snipped fresh cilantro**
- 4 **skinless, boneless chicken breast halves (about 1½ pounds total)**
- 1 **tablespoon lime juice**
- 1 **teaspoon ground cumin**
  Hot cooked rice (optional)

① For the salsa, in a medium bowl stir together chunky salsa, yellow peach, white peach, and cilantro. Cover and chill until ready to serve.

② Brush chicken with lime juice; sprinkle with cumin. For a charcoal grill, grill chicken on the rack of an uncovered grill directly over medium coals for 12 to 15 minutes or until chicken is tender and no longer pink (170°F), turning once halfway through grilling. (For a gas grill, preheat grill. Reduce heat to medium. Place chicken on grill rack over heat. Cover and grill as above.)

③ If desired, serve chicken on hot cooked rice. Spoon salsa over chicken.

PER SERVING 224 cal, 3 g fat (1 g sat. fat), 98 mg chol, 165 mg sodium, 8 g carb, 2 g fiber, 40 g pro

quick tip White peaches typically taste sweeter and less acidic than yellow peaches. They're not as common as yellow peaches; if you can't find them, using two yellow peaches is perfectly acceptable in this fruity salsa.

Caribbean Grilled Chicken and Summer Vegetables

The sour cream dipping sauces cools the fire of the jerk-glazed chicken and vegetables.

MAKES 4 servings **PREP** 20 minutes **GRILL** 12 minutes

- ¼ **cup bottled Caribbean jerk liquid meat marinade**
- 2 **tablespoons olive oil**
- 2 **yellow and/or green sweet peppers, halved lengthwise, stemmed, and seeded**
- 2 **plum tomatoes, halved lengthwise**
- 1 **zucchini, quartered lengthwise**
- 4 **skinless, boneless chicken breast halves (1 to 1¼ pounds total)**
- ½ **cup light sour cream**
- ½ **teaspoon Jamaican jerk seasoning**
  Jamaican jerk seasoning (optional)

① In a small bowl whisk together jerk meat marinade and olive oil. Brush vegetables with some of the oil mixture; set vegetables aside. Brush remaining oil mixture on chicken.

② For a charcoal grill, grill chicken on the rack of an uncovered grill directly over medium coals for 6 minutes. Turn chicken. Add vegetables to grill; grill for 6 to 9 minutes more or until chicken is no longer pink (170°F) and vegetables are crisp-tender, turning vegetables once halfway through grilling. (For a gas grill, preheat grill. Reduce heat to medium. Place chicken on grill rack over heat. Cover and grill as above, adding vegetables as directed.)

③ Meanwhile, for dipping sauce in a small bowl combine sour cream and ½ teaspoon jerk seasoning. If desired, sprinkle with additional jerk seasoning.

④ To serve, cut chicken and vegetables into bite-size pieces. Serve dipping sauce with chicken and vegetables.

PER SERVING 286 cal, 11 g fat (3 g sat. fat), 74 mg chol, 568 mg sodium, 18 g carb, 2 g fiber, 29 g pro

Caribbean Grilled Chicken and
Summer Vegetables

Grilled Chicken, Spinach, and Pear Pitas

Grilled Chicken, Spinach, and Pear Pitas ♥

Let the chicken rest for 5 to 10 minutes before you slice it to let juices reabsorbed back into the meat. The meat will slice neatly, rather than shred.

MAKES 6 servings **PREP** 15 minutes **GRILL** 12 minutes

- 12 ounces skinless, boneless chicken breast halves
- 1 tablespoon balsamic vinegar
- 3 whole wheat pita bread rounds, halved crosswise
- ¼ cup light mayonnaise
- 1 ounce soft goat cheese (chèvre)
- 1 tablespoon fat-free milk
- 1 teaspoon balsamic vinegar
- 1 green onion, thinly sliced
- 1½ cups fresh spinach leaves
- 1 pear or apple, cored and thinly sliced

① Brush chicken on both sides with some of the 1 tablespoon balsamic vinegar. For a charcoal grill, place chicken on the rack of an uncovered grill directly over medium coals. Grill for 12 to 15 minutes or until chicken is no longer pink (170°F), turning once and brushing with the remainder of the 1 tablespoon vinegar halfway through grilling. (For a gas grill, preheat grill. Reduce heat to medium. Place chicken on the grill rack over heat. Cover and grill as above.) Cut each chicken breast half into ½-inch-thick slices.

② Meanwhile, wrap pita bread rounds in foil. Place on the grill rack directly over medium coals. Grill about 8 minutes or until bread is warm, turning once halfway through grilling.

③ For sauce, in a small bowl use a fork to stir together mayonnaise, goat cheese, milk, and 1 teaspoon vinegar. Stir in green onion.

④ To assemble, arrange spinach, pear slices, and chicken in pita bread halves. Spoon about 1 tablespoon sauce into each pita.

PER SERVING 216 cal, 6 g fat (2 g sat. fat), 39 mg chol, 293 mg sodium, 24 g carb, 3 g fiber, 18 g pro

Grilled Chicken with Brown Rice

Very simple but fresh, the chunky tomato-corn-bean salsa for this grilled chicken provides color and crunch for this super-quick dish.

MAKES 4 servings **PREP** 15 minutes **GRILL** 12 minutes

- ½ cup chopped tomato
- ½ cup corn
- ¼ cup canned black beans, rinsed and drained
- 1 tablespoon fresh cilantro
- 1 tablespoon lemon juice
   Salt
- 4 skinless, boneless chicken breast halves
   Salt and black pepper
- 3 cups cooked brown rice

① For the salsa, in a medium bowl stir together tomato, corn, beans, cilantro, and lemon juice; season to taste with salt.

② Season chicken with salt and pepper. For a charcoal grill, place chicken on the rack of an uncovered grill directly over medium coals. Grill for 12 to 15 minutes or until chicken is tender and no longer pink (170°F), turning once halfway through grilling. (For a gas grill, preheat grill. Reduce heat to medium. Place chicken on grill rack over heat. Cover and grill as above.)

③ Spoon salsa on chicken and serve rice on the side.

PER SERVING 323 cal, 4 g fat (1 g sat. fat), 73 mg chol, 201 mg sodium, 41 g carb, 4 g fiber, 29 g pro

Grilled Chicken Sliders ♥

One slider per person can be part of an appetizer buffet, while two sliders per person makes a hearty meal.

MAKES 6 servings **PREP** 20 minutes **GRILL** 10 minutes

- 1 pound skinless chicken breasts
  Salt and black pepper
- 4 kiwifruit, peeled and chopped
- 1 tablespoon chopped fresh mint
- 1 teaspoon honey
- 6 whole wheat cocktail buns, split
- 3 tablespoons honey mustard
- 1 large red apple, cut into 12 thin slices

① Cut chicken breasts in half (for 6 pieces). Place each chicken piece between two pieces of plastic wrap. Using a flat side of a meat mallet, lightly pound the chicken to about ¼-inch thickness. Remove plastic wrap. Season chicken with salt and pepper.

② For a charcoal grill, grill chicken on the rack of an uncovered grill directly over medium coals for 10 to 12 minutes or until chicken is tender and no longer pink (170°F), turning once halfway through grilling. (For a gas grill, preheat grill. Reduce heat to medium. Place chicken on grill rack over heat. Cover and grill as above.)

③ Meanwhile, for chutney, in a small bowl combine kiwi, mint, and honey. Season with salt and pepper. Spread bottom buns with honey mustard and add 2 apple slices. Top with chicken, chutney, and bun tops.

PER SERVING 218 cal, 3 g fat (1 g sat. fat), 44 mg chol, 305 mg sodium, 27 g carb, 4 g fiber, 21 g pro

Grilled Rosemary Chicken ♥

The quickest way to strip rosemary leaves from the stems is to hold the top of the sprig with one hand, then grasp the top leaves with the other and pull down the stem with your fingers. The leaves will come right off!

MAKES 6 servings **PREP** 15 minutes **MARINATE** 1 hour Grill **10 MINUTES**

- 6 medium skinless, boneless chicken breast halves (about 1¾ pounds total)
- 1 teaspoon finely shredded lime peel
- ½ cup lime juice
- 1 tablespoon chopped fresh rosemary
- 1 tablespoon olive oil
- 2 teaspoons sugar
- 2 cloves garlic, minced
- ¼ teaspoon salt
- ⅛ teaspoon black pepper

① Place chicken breast halves between two pieces of plastic wrap. Using the flat side of a meat mallet, lightly pound to an even ½-inch thickness. Place in a large resealable plastic bag set in a shallow dish.

② For marinade, in a small bowl stir together lime peel, lime juice, rosemary, oil, sugar, garlic, and salt. Pour over chicken. Seal bag; turn to coat chicken. Marinate in the refrigerator for 1 to 4 hours, turning bag occasionally.

③ Remove chicken from marinade, discarding marinade. Season chicken with pepper. For a charcoal grill, grill chicken on the grill rack of an uncovered grill directly over medium coals for 10 to 12 minutes or until tender and no longer pink (170°F), turning once halfway through grilling. (For a gas grill, preheat grill. Reduce heat to medium. Place chicken on grill rack over heat. Cover and grill as above.)

PER SERVING 162 cal, 3 g fat (1 g sat. fat), 77 mg chol, 135 mg sodium, 2 g carb, 0 g fiber, 31 g pro

Mushroom-Plum Chicken Kabobs

Mushroom-Plum Chicken Kabobs

Plums are at their peak in late summer or early fall.

MAKES 8 servings **PREP** 15 minutes **GRILL** 12 minutes

- 1 pound skinless, boneless chicken breast halves, cut into 1-inch cubes
- 16 button mushrooms
- 8 green onions, cut into 1½-inch pieces
- 4 firm, ripe plums or 3 peaches, cut into wedges
- ¼ cup balsamic vinegar
- 2 tablespoons canola oil
- ¼ teaspoon salt and freshly ground pepper

① On eight 12-inch metal or wood skewers (see quick tip, page 177), alternately thread chicken, mushrooms, green onions, and plums.

② In a small bowl stir together vinegar and oil; brush on kabobs.

③ For a charcoal grill, grill kabobs on the rack of an uncovered grill directly over medium coals for 12 to 15 minutes or until chicken is tender and no longer pink (170°F), turning once halfway through grilling time. (For a gas grill, preheat grill. Reduce heat to medium. Place skewers on a grill rack over heat. Cover and grill as above.)

④ Transfer kabobs to serving platter; sprinkle with salt and freshly ground pepper.

PER SERVING 122 cal, 4 g fat (0 g sat. fat), 33 mg chol, 114 mg sodium, 7 g carb, 1 g fiber, 14 g pro

Barbecue Glazed Turkey ♥

When you are really short on time, use a favorite bottled barbecue sauce and simply use the recommended timings to grill the meat.

MAKES 4 servings **START TO FINISH** 30 minutes

- ⅔ cup reduced-sugar ketchup or regular ketchup
- ¼ cup orange juice
- 3 tablespoons snipped fresh cilantro
- 1 clove garlic, minced
- ¼ teaspoon ground cumin
- ¼ teaspoon black pepper
- 1 turkey breast tenderloin (about 1 pound), split in half horizontally; or 4 skinless, boneless chicken breast halves (1 to 1¼ pounds total)

① For sauce, in a small saucepan combine ketchup, orange juice, 2 tablespoons of the cilantro, the garlic, cumin, and black pepper. Bring to boiling over medium heat, stirring constantly. Reduce heat. Simmer, uncovered, for 5 minutes. Transfer ⅓ cup of the sauce to a small bowl and keep remaining sauce warm.

② For a charcoal grill, grill turkey pieces on the rack of an uncovered grill directly over medium coals for 12 to 16 minutes or until turkey is tender and no longer pink (170°F), turning once halfway through grilling and brushing with the ⅓ cup sauce for the last 2 minutes of grilling. (For a gas grill, preheat grill. Reduce heat to medium. Place poultry pieces on grill rack over heat. Cover and grill as above.)

③ Slice turkey and serve with remaining sauce. Garnish with remaining 1 tablespoon cilantro.

PER SERVING 163 cal, 1 g fat (0 g sat. fat), 70 mg chol, 298 mg sodium, 10 g carb, 0 g fiber, 28 g pro

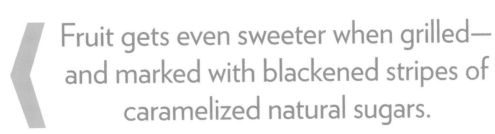

Fruit gets even sweeter when grilled— and marked with blackened stripes of caramelized natural sugars.

Turkey Burger with Peaches and Blueberries

A warm fruit relish of chili powder-spiced peaches and blueberries provides flavor and color on these open-faced burgers.

MAKES 4 servings **PREP** 15 minutes **GRILL** 14 minutes

- 4 small peaches
- 1 pound ground turkey
  Salt and black pepper
- 4 slices Monterey Jack cheese
- ½ cup blueberries
- ¼ teaspoon chili powder
- 4 thick slices roasted garlic country bread or garlic bread, toasted if desired
  Fresh mint (optional)
  Chili powder (optional)

① Finely chop 1 of the peaches; place in a medium bowl. Add ground turkey, salt, and pepper. Shape into four ½-inch-thick patties (if necessary, dampen hands first).

② For a charcoal grill, grill directly over medium-high heat for 4 to 5 minutes per side or until no pink remains (165°F). Add cheese; cover and grill 1 minute. (For a gas grill, preheat grill; reduce heat to medium. Place patties on grill rack directly over heat. Cover and grill as above.)

③ Meanwhile, coarsely chop remaining peaches; combine in a large skillet with blueberries and chili powder. Cook, stirring occasionally, over medium heat for 5 to 6 minutes or until heated through and beginning to have juices form.

④ Top each piece of garlic bread with 1 patty and some of the peach mixture. Add mint and additional chili powder, if desired.

PER SERVING 464 cal, 25 g fat (10 g sat. fat), 114 mg chol, 614 mg sodium, 28 g carb, 3 g fiber, 31 g pro

quick tip Grilled turkey burgers can go from delicious to dried out very easily. While ground turkey breast is the leanest type of ground turkey, use regular ground turkey for these burgers to ensure they stay juicy.

Grilled Turkey Gyros

The Cucumber-Yogurt Sauce for these Greek-inspired sandwiches can be made several hours ahead—and so can the patties. Just be sure to cover them with plastic wrap and refrigerate until you're ready to grill.

MAKES 4 servings **PREP** 20 minutes **GRILL** 6 minutes

- 12 ounces uncooked ground turkey breast
- ¼ cup finely chopped onion
- 1 egg, lightly beaten
- 1 tablespoon fine dry bread crumbs
- 2 cloves garlic, minced
- 1 teaspoon ground coriander
- ½ teaspoon ground cumin
- ⅛ teaspoon salt
- ⅛ teaspoon black pepper
- 1 tablespoon olive oil
- 4 whole wheat pita bread rounds
- 1 cup thinly sliced cucumber
- 1 cup diced tomato
- 2 tablespoons snipped fresh parsley
- 1 recipe Cucumber-Yogurt Sauce

① For patties, in a large bowl combine turkey breast, onion, egg, bread crumbs, garlic, coriander, cumin, salt, and pepper. Shape into 12 patties, flattening each to about ½-inch thickness. Brush all sides of the patties with olive oil; set aside. Wrap pita bread rounds in foil.

② For a charcoal grill, place patties and foil-wrapped pita bread on the greased grill rack directly over medium coals. Grill, uncovered, about 6 minutes or until done (165°F) and pitas are heated through, turning once halfway through grilling. (For a gas grill, preheat grill; reduce heat to medium. Place patties and foil-wrapped pita bread on grill rack directly over heat. Cover and grill as above.)

③ Divide cucumber slices among grilled pita bread rounds. Top each with 3 patties, ¼ cup tomato, and parsley. Drizzle with Cucumber-Yogurt Sauce. Fold pitas around fillings; secure with toothpicks.

Cucumber-Yogurt Sauce: In a small bowl combine ⅓ cup plain fat-free yogurt; ¼ cup shredded, seeded cucumber; 1 tablespoon tahini (sesame seed paste); 2 cloves garlic, minced; and ⅛ teaspoon salt. Cover and refrigerate for at least 20 minutes.

PER SERVING 332 cal, 9 g fat (1 g sat. fat), 95 mg chol, 560 mg sodium, 37 g carb, 6 g fiber, 31 g pro

**Catfish with Summer
Succotash Salad**

Catfish with Summer Succotash Salad

Although catfish just seems to go naturally with succotash, you can substitute other white fish in this recipe—such as tilapia.

MAKES 4 servings **PREP** 15 minutes **GRILL** 6 minutes

- 2 cups frozen lima beans
- 4 4- to 6-ounce catfish fillets, about ½ inch thick
  Olive oil
  Garlic salt and black pepper
- 1 cup purchased corn relish
- 1 cup fresh baby spinach

① Cook lima beans according to package directions. Drain in colander; rinse under cold water to quick cool.

② Meanwhile, rinse fish and pat dry with paper towels. Brush fish with oil and sprinkle with garlic salt and pepper. Place in a well greased grill basket. For a charcoal grill, place grill basket on grill rack directly over medium coals. Grill for 6 to 9 minutes or until fish flakes easily when tested with a fork, turning basket once halfway through grilling. (For a gas grill, preheat grill. Reduce heat to medium. Place grill basket on grill rack directly over heat; cover and grill as above.)

③ Place fish on serving platter. In a large bowl toss together cooked beans, corn relish, and spinach. Serve with fish.

PER SERVING 372 cal, 12 g fat (3 g sat. fat), 53 mg chol, 509 mg sodium, 41 g carb, 5 g fiber, 24 g pro

quick tip If you'd like, you can substitute cooked edamame (green soybeans) for the lima beans.

Grilled Cod with Red Pepper Sauce ♥

If you have reluctant fish-eaters in your family, tempt them with cod, a firm and meaty, mild flavor fish that takes to all kinds of preparations. Start out simply, if necessary, with a bit of butter and a squeeze of fresh lemon. It's hard not to like!

MAKES 4 servings **PREP** 25 minutes **GRILL** 4 minutes

- 4 4- to 6-ounce fresh or frozen skinless cod fillets
- 1¼ cups chopped red sweet pepper (1 large)
- 1 tablespoon olive oil
- 1 cup peeled, seeded, and chopped tomatoes (2 medium)
- 2 tablespoons white wine vinegar
- ¼ teaspoon salt
  Dash cayenne pepper
- 1 tablespoon olive oil
- 1 tablespoon snipped fresh basil or oregano or ½ teaspoon dried basil or oregano, crushed
  Red and/or yellow cherry tomatoes (optional)
  Fresh basil or oregano sprigs (optional)

① Thaw fish, if frozen. Rinse fish; pat dry with paper towels. Measure thickness of fish; set aside.

② For sauce, in a small skillet cook sweet pepper in 1 tablespoon hot oil over medium heat for 3 to 5 minutes or until tender, stirring occasionally. Stir in chopped tomatoes, 1 tablespoon of the vinegar, the salt, and cayenne pepper. Cook about 5 minutes or until tomatoes are softened, stirring occasionally. Cool slightly. Transfer to a blender or food processor. Cover and blend until smooth. Return sauce to skillet; cover and keep warm.

③ In a small bowl stir together the remaining 1 tablespoon vinegar, 1 tablespoon oil, and snipped fresh or dried basil; brush over both sides of fish. Place fish in a greased grill basket, tucking under any thin edges.

④ For a charcoal grill, grill fish in basket on the rack of an uncovered grill directly over medium coals until fish begins to flake when tested with a fork, turning basket once halfway through grilling. Allow 4 to 6 minutes per ½-inch thickness of fish. (For a gas grill, preheat grill. Reduce heat to medium. Place fish in basket on grill rack over heat. Cover and grill as directed.)

⑤ Serve fish with sauce. If desired, garnish with cherry tomatoes and fresh basil sprigs.

PER SERVING 194 cal, 8 g fat (1 g sat. fat), 41 mg chol, 223 mg sodium, 4 g carb, 1 g fiber, 26 g pro

Tilapia Tacos with Jalapeño Slaw ♥

Tacos don't get much lighter and fresher than these fish tacos with a crunchy, citrus vinaigrette-dressed slaw.

MAKES 4 servings **PREP** 20 minutes **GRILL** 4 minutes

- 1 pound fresh or frozen tilapia fillets
- 2½ cups purchased shredded cabbage with carrot (coleslaw mix)
- ¼ cup thinly sliced, halved red onion
- 1 fresh jalapeño, seeded and finely chopped (see quick tip, page 47)
- 2 tablespoons lime juice
- 2 tablespoons orange juice
- 2 tablespoons olive oil
- 1 teaspoon ground cumin
- ⅛ teaspoon salt
- ¼ teaspoon ancho chili powder or cayenne pepper
- 4 whole grain flour tortillas
  Peach or mango salsa (optional)
  Lime wedges

① Thaw fish, if frozen. Rinse fish; pat dry with paper towels. Measure thickness of fish fillets. Set aside. For dressing, in a medium bowl combine coleslaw mix, red onion, and jalapeño; set aside. In a small bowl whisk together lime juice, orange juice, oil, half the cumin, and half the salt. Pour dressing on the cabbage slaw. Toss to coat. Cover and chill until ready to serve.

② In a small bowl combine the remaining cumin, remaining salt, and ancho chili powder; sprinkle evenly on one side of each fish fillet.

③ Stack tortillas and wrap in heavy foil. Place fish and tortilla stack on the greased rack of an uncovered grill directly over medium coals. Grill for 4 to 6 minutes or until fish flakes easily when tested with a fork and tortillas are heated through, turning fish and tortilla stack once halfway through grilling. (For a gas grill, preheat grill. Reduce heat to medium. Place fish and tortilla stack on greased grill rack over heat. Cover and grill as above.)

④ Remove fish and tortillas from grill. Cut fish into 4 serving-size pieces and divide among tortillas. Top with slaw. If desired, serve with salsa and lime wedges.

PER SERVING 324 cal, 12 g fat (3 g sat. fat), 57 mg chol, 466 mg sodium, 21 g carb, 12 g fiber, 32 g pro

Grilled Tuna Sandwiches with Giardiniera Rémoulade

Rémoulade is a French mayonnaise sauce that's given an interesting and acidic bite with mustard, capers, pickles, herbs, and anchovies. This version calls on the Italian mix of vinegary vegetables called *giardiniera* to accomplish the same thing. Use either hot or mild giardiniera, whichever you prefer.

MAKES 4 servings **PREP** 20 minutes **GRILL** 7 minutes

- 1 recipe Giardiniera Rémoulade
- 4 4 to 6-ounce fresh or frozen tuna steaks, cut about ¾ inch thick
- 2 tablespoons garlic flavor oil or 2 tablespoons olive oil and ⅛ teaspoon minced garlic
  Salt
  Black pepper
- ½ of a 12-inch Italian flatbread (focaccia)
- 1 medium tomato, thinly sliced
- 1½ cups torn mesclun or mixed baby salad greens

① Prepare the Giardiniera Rémoulade. Refrigerate until ready to assemble sandwiches.

② Thaw fish, if frozen. Rinse fish; pat dry with paper towels. Brush both sides of fish with oil. Sprinkle with salt and pepper. If desired, place fish in a greased grill basket.

③ For a charcoal grill, grill fish on the greased rack of an uncovered grill directly over medium coals for 6 to 9 minutes or just until fish begins to flake easily when tested with a fork, turning once halfway through grilling. (For a gas grill, preheat grill. Reduce heat to medium. Place fish on greased grill rack over heat. Cover and grill as above.) Remove from grill.

④ Meanwhile, cut flatbread in half. Cut each portion in half horizontally. Add flatbread, cut sides down, to grill. Grill for 1 to 2 minutes or until light brown.

⑤ To assemble, line toasted sides of flatbread with tomato. Top with mesclun, fish, and some of the Giardiniera Rémoulade. Pass the remaining rémoulade.

Giardiniera Rémoulade: In a small bowl combine ⅓ cup drained giardiniera; ⅓ cup fat-free mayonnaise or salad dressing; 3 tablespoons chopped pitted green olives; 3 cloves garlic, minced; ½ teaspoon finely shredded lemon peel; and ¼ teaspoon black pepper.

PER SERVING 510 cal, 13 g fat (3 g sat. fat), 19 mg chol, 813 mg sodium, 56 g carb, 5 g fiber, 42 g pro

Grilled Tuna Sandwiches with
Giardiniera Rémoulade

Easy Salmon Burgers

Easy Salmon Burgers

Slices of cool, buttery avocado are a delicious contrast to the warm, crisp-crusted salmon burgers.

MAKES 4 servings **PREP** 25 minutes **GRILL** 6 minutes

- 1 cup broken Italian herbed crisp flatbread crackers (8 crackers)
- 1 pound skinless, boneless salmon fillets, cut into 2-inch pieces
- 1 egg
- 3 tablespoons Dijon mustard or honey mustard
- 4 ciabatta buns, split
  Sliced avocado and green onions (optional)

① In food processor, place crackers. Cover and process until coarsely ground. Add half the salmon, the egg, and 1 tablespoon of the mustard. Cover and process until salmon is ground and mixture is thoroughly combined. Add remaining salmon. Cover and pulse with several on/off turns until salmon is coarsely chopped. With damp hands, shape into four ½-inch-thick patties.

② Lightly brush patties with olive oil. Grill directly on a greased grill rack over medium heat 3 minutes per side or until cooked through (160°F). Grill buns, cut sides down, the last 1 to 2 minutes of grilling. (For a gas grill, preheat grill. Reduce heat to medium. Cover and grill as above.)

③ Serve salmon patties on buns with sliced avocado and green onions.

PER SERVING 614 cal, 23 g fat (5 g sat. fat), 120 mg chol, 968 mg sodium, 67 g carb, 3 g fiber, 36 g pro

quick tip Only pulse the salmon in the food processor as long as it takes to get it to a medium-coarse grind. Over-processing the salmon can make it tough.

Grilled Salmon with Tomato-Ginger Relish

Finely chopping 6 cups of cherry tomatoes is probably the most time-consuming part of this recipe. It's easily done in a food processor, if you like.

MAKES 8 to 10 servings **PREP** 20 minutes **GRILL** 13 minutes

- 6 cups red and/or yellow cherry tomatoes, finely chopped
- 3 tablespoons white balsamic vinegar or white wine vinegar
- 1 tablespoon grated fresh ginger
- 2 teaspoons salt
- 2 3 to 3½-pound fresh or frozen whole salmon fillets with skin
- 1 tablespoon olive oil
- ½ teaspoon freshly ground black pepper
- 3 tablespoons fresh thyme leaves
  Fresh thyme sprigs (optional)
  Lime wedges (optional)

① For relish, in a medium bowl combine tomatoes, vinegar, ginger, and 1 teaspoon of the salt. Set aside.

② Thaw fish, if frozen. Rinse fish; pat dry with paper towels. Brush both sides of fish with oil. Sprinkle with the remaining salt and the pepper. Sprinkle the thyme leaves on skinned side of fish; press gently with your fingers.

③ For a charcoal grill, grill 1 of the fish fillets, skin side up, on the rack of an uncovered grill directly over medium coals for 8 to 10 minutes or until light brown. Using 2 large metal spatulas, carefully turn fish. Grill for 5 to 10 minutes more or until fish flakes easily when tested with a fork. (For a gas grill, preheat grill. Reduce heat to medium. Place 1 fish fillet, skin side up, on grill rack over heat. Cover and grill as above.) Transfer fish to a serving platter; cover and keep warm. Clean grill rack. Grill remaining fish fillet.

④ Serve fish with relish. If desired, garnish with thyme sprigs and serve with lime wedges.

PER SERVING 756 cal, 48 g fat (11 g sat. fat), 187 mg chol, 790 mg sodium, 7 g carb, 2 g fiber, 71 g pro

Shrimp and Chorizo Kabobs

Ancho chiles are dried poblano peppers, the deep-green fresh chiles that are stuffed with cheese, battered, and deep-fried to make chiles rellenos. If you can't find ground ancho chile pepper in your supermarket, look for it in a Mexican food market.

MAKES 8 servings **PREP** 20 minutes **GRILL** 4 minutes
MARINATE 30 minutes

- 2 pounds fresh or frozen jumbo shrimp (about 40 shrimp total)
- ¼ cup olive oil
- 2 tablespoons ground ancho chile pepper
- 1 teaspoon salt
- ⅛ teaspoon ground chipotle chile pepper
- 3 cloves garlic, minced
- 12 ounces cooked smoked chorizo sausage, cut into ½-inch slices (about 40 slices)

① Thaw shrimp, if frozen. Peel and devein shrimp. Rinse shrimp; pat dry with paper towels. In a large bowl combine olive oil, ancho chile pepper, salt, chipotle chile pepper, and garlic. Mix well. Add shrimp; toss to coat. Cover bowl with plastic wrap; marinate in the refrigerator for 30 minutes (do not marinate any longer).

② Drain shrimp, discarding marinade. Tuck 1 slice of chorizo into the crook of 1 shrimp and thread onto a 12-inch skewer, making sure the skewer goes through one side of the shrimp, the chorizo, and the other side of the shrimp. Divide ingredients evenly among 8 skewers.

③ For a charcoal grill, grill kabobs on the rack of an uncovered grill directly over medium-hot coals for 4 to 6 minutes or until shrimp are opaque, turning once halfway through grilling. (For a gas grill, preheat grill. Reduce heat to medium. Add kabobs to grill rack. Cover and grill as above.)

PER SERVING 392 cal, 27 g fat (9 g sat. fat), 210 mg chol, 1,209 mg sodium, 1 g carb, 0 g fiber, 34 g pro

Couscous and Squash ♥

The head of cauliflower is cut into thick slices to make it easy to grill. After it's cooked, break or cut the slices and florets into pieces.

MAKES 4 servings **PREP** 25 minutes **GRILL** 5 minutes

- ¼ cup lime juice
- 3 tablespoons olive oil
- ½ teaspoon salt
- ½ teaspoon ground cumin
- ½ teaspoon black pepper
- 2 small zucchini and/or yellow summer squash
- 1 small head cauliflower, trimmed
- 1 small red onion
- 1½ cups water
- 1 cup couscous
- 1 teaspoon finely shredded lime peel
  Snipped fresh parsley (optional)

① In a small bowl whisk together lime juice, oil, salt, cumin, and pepper; set aside.

② Cut zucchini lengthwise into ½-inch-thick slices. Cut cauliflower crosswise into 4 equal slices. Cut red onion crosswise into ½-inch-thick slices. Brush vegetable slices with some of the oil mixture.

③ For a charcoal grill, grill vegetables on the rack of an uncovered grill directly over medium coals until crisp-tender, carefully turning vegetables once with a wide spatula halfway through grilling. Allow 5 to 6 minutes for zucchini and 10 to 12 minutes for cauliflower and onion. (For a gas grill, preheat grill. Reduce heat to medium. Place vegetables on grill rack over heat. Cover and grill as above.)

④ Meanwhile, in a small saucepan bring the water to boiling. Stir in couscous and lime peel. Remove from heat; let stand, covered, for 5 minutes. Fluff couscous with a fork.

⑤ To serve, drizzle vegetables and couscous with the remaining oil mixture. If desired, sprinkle with parsley.

PER SERVING 311 cal, 11 g fat (2 g sat. fat), 0 mg chol, 335 mg sodium, 46 g carb, 6 g fiber, 9 g pro

For families busy with a multitude of tasks, errands, and activities, this is the way to cook: Put the ingredients in a slow cooker, cover, and turn it on—then get a dozen things done while dinner cooks the no-tend way.

214

218

225

SLOW & SIMPLE

234

Cincinnati Chili

Yes, that's chocolate in there. Cincinnati-style chili is defined by sweet spices—such as cinnamon (and sometimes chocolate)—and the bed of spaghetti on which it's served.

MAKES 6 servings **PREP** 30 minutes
COOK 8 hours (low) or 4 hours (high)

- 1 **bay leaf**
- ½ **teaspoon whole allspice**
- ½ **teaspoon whole cloves**
- 2 **pounds lean ground beef**
- 2 **cups chopped onions (2 large)**
- 1 **15-ounce can dark red kidney beans, rinsed and drained**
- 1 **15-ounce can tomato sauce**
- 1½ **cups water**
- 3 **tablespoons chili powder**
- 4 **cloves garlic, minced**
- 1 **teaspoon Worcestershire sauce**
- ¾ **teaspoon ground cumin**
- ¾ **teaspoon ground cinnamon**
- ½ **teaspoon salt**
- ¼ **teaspoon cayenne pepper**
- ½ **ounce unsweetened chocolate, chopped**
- 12 **ounces dried spaghetti, cooked and drained**
- 1 **cup shredded cheddar cheese (4 ounces)**

① For a spice bag, cut a 4-inch square from a double thickness of 100%-cotton cheesecloth. Place bay leaf, allspice, and cloves in the center of the cheesecloth square. Bring up corners of cheesecloth, tie closed with 100%-cotton kitchen string, and set aside.

② In a large skillet cook ground beef over medium heat until brown, using a spoon to break up meat as it cooks. Drain off fat. Transfer meat to a 3½- or 4-quart slow cooker. Stir onions, beans, tomato sauce, the water, chili powder, garlic, Worcestershire sauce, cumin, cinnamon, salt, and cayenne pepper into meat in cooker. Add spice bag.

③ Cover and cook on low-heat setting for 8 to 10 hours or on high-heat setting for 4 to 5 hours, stirring in chocolate during the last 30 minutes of cooking time.

④ To serve, remove spice bag. Spoon chili over hot cooked spaghetti. Sprinkle each serving with cheese.

PER SERVING 743 cal, 32 g fat (14 g sat. fat), 123 mg chol, 953 mg sodium, 69 g carb, 10 g fiber, 48 g pro

Curried Chicken Stew

Bone-in chicken thighs are a perfect match for the slow cooker—they stay nice and juicy, even after hours of cooking.

MAKES 4 servings **PREP** 20 minutes
COOK 7 hours (low) or 3½ hours (high)

- 8 **bone-in chicken thighs (2½ to 3 pounds)**
- 2 **teaspoons olive oil**
- 6 **carrots, cut in 2-inch pieces**
- 1 **medium sweet onion, cut in thin wedges**
- 1 **cup unsweetened coconut milk**
- ¼ **cup mild or hot curry paste**
  Chopped pistachios, golden raisins, cilantro, and/or crushed red pepper (optional)

① Trim excess skin and fat from chicken thighs (or remove skin, if desired). In a 12-inch skillet cook chicken, skin side down, in hot olive oil for 8 minutes, or until browned. (Do not turn thighs.) Remove from heat; drain and discard fat.

② In a 3½- or 4-quart slow cooker combine carrots and onion. In a bowl whisk together half the coconut milk and the curry paste; pour over carrots and onion (refrigerate remaining coconut milk). Place chicken, skin side up, on vegetables. Cover and cook on low for 7 to 8 hours or on high for 3½ to 4 hours.

③ Remove chicken from slow cooker. Skim off excess fat from sauce in cooker, then stir in remaining coconut milk.

④ Serve stew in bowls. If desired, top each serving with pistachios, raisins, cilantro, and/or crushed red pepper.

PER SERVING 850 cal, 63 g fat (25 g sat. fat), 238 mg chol, 1314 mg sodium, 21 g carb, 5 g fiber, 52 g pro

quick tip Curry is from the Southern India term kari, meaning sauce and refers to hot, spicy gravy-based dishes of Easy Indian origin. Curry paste is available green (sweet but as hot as red curry), yellow (more mild and rich) and red (hot).

Chicken Fajita Chili

Chicken Fajita Chili ♥

Here are all the flavors of a platter of sizzling fajitas, simmering on your countertop—ready and waiting when you come home for dinner.

MAKES 6 servings **PREP** 25 minutes
COOK 4 hours (low) or 2 hours (high)

- 2 pounds skinless, boneless chicken breast halves, cut into 1-inch pieces
- 1 tablespoon chili powder
- 1 teaspoon fajita seasoning
- 2 cloves garlic, minced
- ½ teaspoon ground cumin
  Nonstick cooking spray
- 2 14.5-ounce cans no-salt-added diced tomatoes, undrained
- 1 16-ounce package frozen yellow, green, and red peppers and onions
- 1 19-ounce can cannellini beans (white kidney beans), rinsed and drained
- 3 tablespoons shredded reduced-fat cheddar cheese (optional)
- 3 tablespoons light sour cream (optional)
- 3 tablespoons guacamole (optional)

① In a medium bowl combine chicken, chili powder, fajita seasoning, garlic, and cumin; toss gently to coat. Set aside. Coat a large skillet with cooking spray; heat skillet over medium-high heat. Cook half the chicken at a time in hot skillet until brown, stirring occasionally. Transfer to a 3½- or 4-quart slow cooker.

② Stir tomatoes, frozen vegetables, and beans into chicken in slow cooker.

③ Cover and cook on low-heat setting for 4 to 5 hours or on high-heat setting for 2 to 2½ hours. If desired, top each serving with cheese, sour cream, and guacamole.

PER SERVING 261 cal, 2 g fat (1 g sat. fat), 88 mg chol, 294 mg sodium, 22 g carb, 7 g fiber, 41 g pro

Chicken and Shrimp Jambalaya ♥

Shrimp are added at the very end of cooking time to heat through while staying tender with delicate texture.

MAKES 8 servings **PREP** 20 minutes
COOK 4½ hours (low) + 30 minutes (high) or 2¼ hours (high)

- 1 pound skinless, boneless chicken breast halves or thighs
- 2 cups thinly sliced celery (4 stalks)
- 2 cups chopped onions (2 large)
- 1 14.5-ounce can no-salt-added diced tomatoes, undrained
- 1 14.5-ounce can reduced-sodium chicken broth
- ½ 6-ounce can no-salt-added tomato paste (⅓ cup)
- 1½ teaspoons Homemade Salt-Free Cajun Seasoning or 1½ teaspoons salt-free Cajun seasoning
- 2 cloves garlic, minced
- ½ teaspoon salt
- 8 ounces fresh or frozen peeled and deveined cooked shrimp
- 1½ cups uncooked instant brown rice
- ¾ cup chopped green, red, or yellow sweet pepper (1 medium)
- 2 tablespoons snipped fresh parsley
  Celery leaves (optional)

① Cut chicken into ¾-inch pieces. In a 3½- or 4-quart slow cooker combine chicken, celery, onions, tomatoes, broth, tomato paste, Homemade Salt-Free Cajun Seasoning, garlic, and salt.

② Cover and cook on low-heat setting for 4½ to 5½ hours or on high-heat setting for 2¼ to 2¾ hours.

③ Thaw shrimp, if frozen; set aside. If using low-heat setting, turn to high-heat setting. Stir in uncooked brown rice and sweet pepper. Cover and cook for about 30 minutes more or until most of the liquid is absorbed and rice is tender.

④ Before serving, stir shrimp and parsley into jambalaya. If desired, garnish with celery leaves.

Homemade Salt-Free Cajun Seasoning: In a small bowl stir together ¼ teaspoon ground white pepper, ¼ teaspoon garlic powder, ¼ teaspoon onion powder, ¼ teaspoon paprika, ¼ teaspoon ground black pepper, and ⅛ to ¼ teaspoon cayenne pepper.

PER SERVING 211 cal, 2 g fat (0 g sat. fat), 88 mg chol, 415 mg sodium, 26 g carb, 4 g fiber, 23 g pro

Moroccan-Spiced Chicken Lentil Stew ♥

Browning the chicken before putting it in the slow cooker with the other ingredients gives it better flavor and color after it's cooked.

MAKES 8 servings **PREP** 30 minutes
COOK 7 hours (low) + 15 minutes (high) or 3½ hours (high)

- 2 pounds skinless, boneless chicken thighs
- 2 cloves garlic, minced
- ½ teaspoon ground cumin
- ½ teaspoon ground coriander
- ¼ teaspoon black pepper
- ¼ teaspoon ground cinnamon
   Nonstick cooking spray
- 1¼ cups dry brown lentils, rinsed and drained
- 1 medium onion, cut into thin wedges
- 2 14-ounce cans reduced-sodium chicken broth
- 1 cup water
- 1 large yellow summer squash, quartered lengthwise and cut into 1-inch-thick pieces
- ½ cup snipped dried apricots or golden raisins
   Sliced green onions (optional)

① Trim fat from chicken. Cut chicken into 2- to 3-inch chunks. In a large bowl combine chicken, garlic, cumin, coriander, pepper, and cinnamon; toss to coat. Coat a extra-large unheated nonstick skillet with cooking spray. Preheat over medium heat. Add chicken to hot skillet; cook until browned, turning to brown all sides.

② Transfer chicken to a 4- or 5-quart slow cooker. Add lentils and onion to slow cooker. Pour chicken broth and the water over all.

③ Cover and cook on low-heat setting for 7 to 8 hours or on high-heat setting for 3½ to 4 hours. If using low-heat setting, turn to high-heat setting. Add squash and apricots to slow cooker. Cover and cook about 15 minutes more or just until squash is tender. If desired, garnish individual servings with sliced green onions.

PER SERVING 274 cal, 5 g fat (1 g sat. fat), 94 mg chol, 318 mg sodium, 26 g carb, 10 g fiber, 32 g pro

Chili-Style Vegetable Pasta

No one will miss the meat in this hearty meatless meal.

MAKES 6 servings **PREP** 20 minutes
COOK 5 hours (low) or 2½ hours (high)

- 2 14½-ounce cans no-salt-added diced tomatoes, undrained
- 1 15-ounce can garbanzo beans (chickpeas), rinsed and drained
- 1 15-ounce can red kidney beans, rinsed and drained
- 1 8-ounce can tomato sauce
- 1 cup finely chopped onion
- 1 cup chopped green or yellow sweet pepper
- 2 to 3 teaspoons chili powder
- 2 cloves garlic, minced
- ½ teaspoon dried oregano, crushed
- ⅛ teaspoon cayenne pepper
- 8 ounces dried whole wheat penne pasta (2 cups)
- ½ cup shredded reduced-fat cheddar cheese (2 ounces)

① In a 3½- or 4-quart slow cooker combine undrained tomatoes, garbanzo beans, kidney beans, tomato sauce, onion, sweet pepper, chili powder, garlic, oregano, and cayenne pepper. Cover; cook on low-heat setting for 5 to 6 hours or on high-heat setting for 2½ to 3 hours.

② To serve, cook pasta according to package directions; drain. Serve chili over hot cooked pasta. Sprinkle with cheese.

PER SERVING 327 cal, 4 g fat (1 g sat. fat), 7 mg chol, 693 mg sodium, 63 g carb, 12 g fiber, 18 g pro

Chili-Style
Vegetable Pasta

Jalapeño Chicken Breasts

Jalapeño Chicken Breasts 🍲

This chicken dish has the flavors of jalapeño poppers—spicy chiles tempered by a cream cheese sauce—and a topping of crisp-cooked and crumbled bacon to boot.

MAKES 6 servings **PREP** 15 minutes
COOK 5 hours (low) + 15 minutes (high) or 2½ hours (high)

6	bone-in chicken breast halves, skinned
1	tablespoon chili powder
⅛	teaspoon salt
½	cup reduced-sodium chicken broth
2	tablespoons lemon juice
⅓	cup sliced pickled jalapeño, drained
1	tablespoon cornstarch
1	tablespoon cold water
1	8-ounce package reduced-fat cream cheese (Neufchâtel), cut into cubes and softened
2	slices bacon, crisp-cooked, drained, and crumbled (optional)

① Sprinkle chicken with chili powder and salt. Arrange chicken, bone sides down, in a 4½- to 6-quart slow cooker. Pour broth and lemon juice around chicken. Top with drained jalapeño pepper.

② Cover and cook on low-heat setting for 5 to 6 hours or on high-heat setting for 2½ to 3 hours.

③ Transfer chicken and jalapeño pepper to a serving platter, reserving cooking liquid. Cover chicken and keep warm.

④ If using low-heat setting, turn to high-heat setting. For sauce, in a small bowl combine the cornstarch and water; stir into cooking liquid. Add cream cheese, whisking until combined. Cover and cook about 15 minutes more or until thickened. Serve chicken with sauce. If desired, sprinkle with bacon.

PER SERVING 329 cal, 11 g fat (6 g sat. fat), 143 mg chol, 489 mg sodium, 5 g carb, 1 g fiber, 49 g pro

Barbecue-Chutney Chicken

Mango chutney can be hot or mild—choose the level of heat you like.

MAKES 4 to 6 servings
COOK 6 hours (low) or 3 hours (high)

1	medium onion, cut into wedges
3	pounds meaty chicken pieces (breast halves, thighs, and drumsticks), skinned
¼	teaspoon salt
⅛	teaspoon black pepper
½	cup mango chutney
⅔	cup barbecue sauce
1	teaspoon curry powder
2	to 3 cups hot cooked rice
	Finely chopped mango (optional)
	Chopped green onion (optional)

① Place onion in a 3½- or 4-quart slow cooker. Add chicken; sprinkle with salt and pepper. Snip any large pieces of chutney. In a small bowl combine chutney, barbecue sauce, and curry powder. Pour over chicken.

② Cover and cook on low-heat setting for 6 to 7 hours or on high-heat setting for 3 to 3½ hours.

③ If desired, toss rice with chopped mango and/or green onion. Serve chicken and chutney over rice.

PER SERVING 538 cal, 12 g fat (3 g sat. fat), 138 mg chol, 647 mg sodium, 57 g carb, 2 g fiber, 48 g pro

Barbecue-Chutney Chicken

Mu-Shu-Style Chicken Wraps

When you order a mu-shu-style dish at a Chinese restaurant, you get thin pancakes in which to wrap the savory filling. This simple version substitutes tortillas.

MAKES 4 servings **PREP** 25 minutes
COOK 6 hours (low) to 3 hours (high)

2½   to 3 pounds meaty chicken pieces (breast halves, thighs, and drumsticks), skinned
¼   teaspoon salt
⅛   teaspoon black pepper
½   cup water
¼   cup soy sauce
2   teaspoons toasted sesame oil
¾   teaspoon ground ginger
8   7- to 8-inch flour tortillas
½   cup hoisin sauce
2   cups packaged shredded broccoli (broccoli slaw mix) or packaged shredded cabbage with carrot (coleslaw mix)
    Sliced green onions

① Place chicken pieces in a 3½- or 4-quart slow cooker. Sprinkle with salt and pepper. In a small bowl, combine the water, soy sauce, oil, and ginger. Pour over chicken in cooker.

② Cover and cook on low-heat setting for 6 to 7 hours or on high-heat setting for 3 to 3½ hours.

③ Transfer chicken to a cutting board, reserving cooking juices in cooker; cool chicken slightly. Remove chicken from bones. Discard bones. Using two forks, shred chicken. Return chicken to cooker; heat through.

④ Meanwhile, preheat oven to 350°F. Wrap tortillas tightly in foil. Heat in oven for 10 to 15 minutes or until warm and soft.

⑤ To serve, spread each tortilla with 1 tablespoon of the hoisin sauce. Using a slotted spoon, divide chicken among tortillas, placing chicken in center of each tortilla. Top with shredded broccoli. Roll or fold tortillas around filling. Serve with green onions.

PER SERVING 520 cal, 18 g fat (4 g sat. fat), 115 mg chol, 1,315 mg sodium, 44 g carb, 3 g fiber, 44 g pro

Chinese Chicken Salad

Slow-cooked Asian-style chicken is shredded and combined with crunchy vegetables and greens in this refreshingly light salad.

MAKES 6 to 8 servings **PREP** 15 minutes
COOK 5 hours (low) or 2½ hours (high)

2   pounds chicken thighs, skinned
    Black pepper
1   cup chopped celery (2 stalks)
½   cup chopped onion (1 medium)
2   cloves garlic, minced
½   cup bottled hoisin sauce
2   tablespoons reduced-sodium soy sauce
2   tablespoons grated fresh ginger
1   tablespoon dry sherry
2   teaspoons Asian chili sauce
1   teaspoon toasted sesame oil
¼   cup rice vinegar
8   cups shredded romaine lettuce
1   cup shredded carrots (2 medium)
⅓   cup unsalted dry-roasted cashews
2   tablespoons snipped fresh cilantro

① Sprinkle chicken with pepper. Place chicken in a 3½- or 4-quart slow cooker. Add celery, onion, and garlic. In a small bowl combine hoisin sauce, soy sauce, ginger, sherry, chili sauce, and sesame oil. Stir into mixture in cooker.

② Cover and cook on low-heat setting for 5 to 6 hours or on high-heat setting for 2½ to 3 hours.

③ Using a slotted spoon, transfer chicken to a cutting board, reserving ½ cup of the cooking liquid. When chicken is cool enough to handle, remove chicken from bones; discard bones. Shred chicken by pulling two forks through it in opposite directions.

④ For dressing, in a screw-top jar combine the reserved ½ cup cooking liquid and the rice vinegar. Cover and shake until combined; set aside.

⑤ In a large salad bowl combine chicken, romaine, carrots, cashews, and cilantro. Shake dressing and drizzle over salad. Toss to coat.

PER SERVING 230 cal, 9 g fat (2 g sat. fat), 71 mg chol, 584 mg sodium, 16 g carb, 3 g fiber, 21 g pro

Chinese Chicken Salad

Pork Loin with Butternut Squash

Cranberry-Chipotle Country-Style Ribs ♥

These hearty boneless ribs in a spicy-sweet-smoky sauce are delicious with corn bread and crunchy coleslaw.

MAKES 6 to 8 servings **PREP** 15 minutes
COOK 7 hours (low) or 3½ hours (high)

2½ to 3 pounds boneless pork country-style ribs

    Salt

    Black pepper

1 16-ounce can whole cranberry sauce

1 cup chopped onion (1 large)

3 chipotle peppers in adobo sauce, finely chopped

1½ teaspoons bottled minced garlic (3 cloves)

① Trim fat from ribs. Sprinkle ribs with salt and black pepper. Place ribs in a 3½- or 4-quart slow cooker. For sauce, in a medium bowl combine cranberry sauce, onion, chipotle peppers, and garlic. Pour sauce over ribs.

② Cover and cook on low-heat setting for 7 to 8 hours or on high-heat setting for 3½ to 4 hours.

③ Transfer ribs to a serving platter. Stir sauce. Drizzle some of the sauce over ribs. If desired, serve with remaining sauce.

PER SERVING 395 cal, 10 g fat (4 g sat. fat), 139 mg chol, 247 mg sodium, 32 g carb, 2 g fiber, 40 g pro

Jerk Pork Wraps with Lime Mayo

It's perfectly fine to use lower-fat mayonnaise in the Lime Mayo to cut down on a few calories and fat grams.

MAKES 6 servings **PREP** 30 minutes
COOK 8 hours (low) or 4 hours (high)

1 1½- to 2-pound boneless pork shoulder roast

1 tablespoon Jamaican jerk seasoning

1 cup water

¼ teaspoon dried thyme, crushed

1 tablespoon lime juice

6 10-inch flour tortillas

6 lettuce leaves (optional)

½ cup chopped red or green sweet pepper (1 medium)

1 cup chopped fresh mango or pineapple

1 recipe Lime Mayo

① Trim fat from meat. If necessary, cut meat to fit into a 3½- or 4-quart slow cooker. Sprinkle jerk seasoning evenly over meat; rub into meat with your fingers. Place meat in slow cooker. Pour the water over meat in cooker. Sprinkle with thyme.

② Cover and cook on low-heat setting for 8 to 10 hours or on high-heat setting for 4 to 5 hours.

③ Transfer meat to a cutting board; cool meat slightly. Using two forks, shred meat, discarding fat. Place meat in a medium bowl. Stir lime juice into meat.

④ If desired, line tortillas with lettuce leaves. Divide pork among tortillas. Top with sweet pepper, mango, and Lime Mayo. Fold tortillas over filling and fold in sides or roll up.

Lime Mayo: In a small bowl stir together ½ cup mayonnaise or salad dressing, ¼ cup finely chopped red onion, ¼ teaspoon finely shredded lime peel, 1 tablespoon lime juice, and 1 clove minced garlic. Cover and refrigerate until ready to serve or up to 1 week.

PER SERVING 314 cal, 13 g fat (3 g sat. fat), 48 mg chol, 503 mg sodium, 33 g carb, 2 g fiber, 16 g pro

Jerk Pork Wraps with Lime Mayo

Easy Southern-Style Ribs

Both pasilla chile powder and ancho chile powder offer medium heat with a slightly sweet, smoky flavor. Look at Mexican markets for either spice.

MAKES 6 to 8 servings **PREP** 25 minutes
COOK 8 hours (low) or 4 hours (high) **BROIL** 5 minutes

- 4 to 5 pounds pork loin back ribs or meaty pork spareribs, cut into 2- to 3-rib portions
- 1 tablespoon smoked paprika or sweet paprika
- 1½ teaspoons packed brown sugar
- 1 teaspoon ground pasilla chile pepper or ancho chile pepper
- ½ teaspoon salt
- ½ teaspoon garlic powder
- ½ teaspoon ground coriander
- ½ teaspoon dry mustard
- ¼ teaspoon celery salt
- ¼ teaspoon coarsely ground black pepper
- ⅛ teaspoon cayenne pepper
- ½ cup chicken broth
- ¾ cup barbecue sauce

① Trim fat from ribs. For rub, in a small bowl combine paprika, brown sugar, pasilla pepper, salt, garlic powder, coriander, mustard, celery salt, black pepper, and cayenne pepper. Generously sprinkle rub on both sides of ribs; rub in with your fingers. Place ribs in a 5- to 6-quart slow cooker, cutting ribs to fit, if necessary.

② In a small bowl combine broth and ¼ cup of the barbecue sauce. Add to slow cooker.

③ Cover and cook on low-heat setting for 8 to 10 hours or on high-heat setting for 4 to 5 hours.

④ Preheat broiler. Line a baking sheet with foil and transfer ribs, meaty sides up, to prepared baking sheet. Brush with the remaining ½ cup barbecue sauce. Broil 6 to 8 inches from heat for 5 to 8 minutes or until sauce begins to brown.

PER SERVING 584 cal, 44 g fat (16 g sat. fat), 152 mg chol, 831 mg sodium, 13 g carb, 0 g fiber, 30 g pro

Spanish Strata

The protein in eggs makes them bind to the vessel in which they're cooked. Translation: They stick like crazy! Be sure to use a disposable slow cooker liner to prevent having to soak and scrub the cooker.

MAKES 8 servings **PREP** 25 minutes **COOK** 5½ hours (low)
COOL 15 minutes

- Disposable slow cooker liner
- 4 cups country-style bread, cut into 1-inch pieces
- 1½ cups frozen diced hash brown potatoes with onions and peppers
- 1 cup shredded Manchego cheese (4 ounces)
- ½ cup coarsely chopped sweet onion, such as Vidalia or Walla Walla (1 small)
- ½ cup coarsely chopped roasted red sweet pepper
- 2 ounces Serrano ham or cooked smoked chorizo, chopped
- 2 cloves garlic, minced
- 2 cups milk
- 4 eggs or 1 cup refrigerated or thawed frozen egg product
- ½ teaspoon salt
- ¼ teaspoon crushed red pepper

① Line a 3½- or 4-quart slow cooker with a disposable slow cooker liner. In a large bowl combine bread pieces, potatoes, cheese, onion, sweet pepper, ham, and garlic. Spoon bread mixture into prepared cooker. In the same bowl whisk together milk, eggs, salt, and crushed red pepper. Pour egg mixture over bread in cooker.

② Cover and cook on low-heat setting for 5½ to 6 hours. Remove ceramic liner from cooker, if possible, or turn off cooker. Cool strata for 15 to 30 minutes.

③ To unmold strata, run a butter knife around the edge of the disposable liner. Place a large plate over the crockery liner. Using two pot holders, carefully invert strata onto plate. Remove and discard disposable liner. Slice strata to serve.

PER SERVING 230 cal, 11 g fat (5 g sat. fat), 126 mg chol, 569 mg sodium, 20 g carb, 1 g fiber, 13 g pro

Ham and Broccoli Potatoes

Ham and Broccoli Potatoes

The topping for this fast-food favorite cooks itself while you're busy with other chores. Start the potatoes about 1 hour before you're ready to eat.

MAKES 6 servings **PREP** 15 minutes **COOK** 3 hours

- 2 cups shredded Swiss cheese (8 ounces)
- 2 cups loose-pack frozen cut broccoli
- 1½ cups diced cooked ham (8 ounces)
- 1 10.75-ounce can reduced-fat and reduced-sodium condensed cream of celery or cream of chicken soup
- ½ teaspoon caraway seeds
- 6 potatoes, baked and split (see Quick Tip, below)

① In a 1½-quart slow cooker combine cheese, broccoli, ham, soup, and caraway seeds.

② Cover and cook (on low-heat setting if available) for 3 to 4 hours. Stir before serving. Spoon ham and broccoli over baked potatoes.

PER SERVING 387 cal, 13 g fat (8 g sat. fat), 54 mg chol, 836 mg sodium, 45 g carb, 5 g fiber, 23 g pro

---

quick tip Bake the potatoes while the ham-and-broccoli finishes cooking. Preheat oven to 425°F. Scrub potatoes and pat dry. Prick potatoes with a fork. (If desired, for soft skins, rub potatoes with shortening or olive oil, or wrap each potato in foil.) Bake potatoes for 40 to 60 minutes or until tender. Roll each potato gently under your hand. Using a knife, cut an X in each potato. Press in and up on ends of each potato to open and reveal the pulp.

Wild Rice-Ham Soup ♥

Adding vegetables toward the end of cooking time preserves color, texture, flavor—and nutrition.

MAKES 6 servings **PREP** 20 minutes
COOK 6 hours (low) + 30 minutes (high) or 3 hours (high)

- 5 cups water
- 1 14.5-ounce can reduced-sodium chicken broth
- 1 cup chopped celery (2 stalks)
- 1 cup diced cooked ham
- ¾ cup uncooked wild rice, rinsed and drained
- 1 medium onion, cut into thin wedges
- 1½ teaspoons dried thyme, crushed
- 1½ cups chopped red sweet peppers (2 medium)
- 4 cups shredded fresh spinach leaves

① In a 4- to 5-quart slow cooker combine the water, broth, celery, ham, wild rice, onion, and thyme.

② Cover and cook on low-heat setting for 6 to 7 hours or on high-heat setting for 3 to 3½ hours.

③ If using low-heat setting, turn to high-heat setting. Stir in sweet peppers. Cover and cook for 30 minutes more. Before serving, stir in spinach.

PER SERVING 124 cal, 1 g fat (0 g sat. fat), 11 mg chol, 584 mg sodium, 20 g carb, 3 g fiber, 10 g pro

Wild Rice-Ham Soup

Slow-Cooked Beef Fajitas

Salsa verde—the foundation for the sauce in these slow-cooked beef fajitas—is based on tomatillos, which have a slightly citrusy flavor.

MAKES 8 servings **PREP** 25 minutes
COOK 8 hours (low) or 4 hours (high)

1½ pounds beef flank steak

1 large green sweet pepper, cored, seeded, cut into ½-inch-wide slices

1 large red sweet pepper, cored, seeded, cut into ½-inch-wide slices

1 large yellow sweet pepper, cored, seeded, cut into ½-inch-wide slices

1 large onion, sliced

1 16-ounce jar salsa verde (about 1¾ cups)

8 8-inch whole wheat flour tortillas, warmed (see Quick Tip, below)

½ cup light sour cream

① Trim fat from meat. If necessary, cut meat to fit into a 3½- or 4-quart slow cooker. Place peppers and onion into cooker. Top with meat. Pour salsa over meat.

② Cover and cook on low-heat setting for 8 to 10 hours or on high-heat setting for 4 to 5 hours. Transfer meat to a cutting board; use two forks to pull meat apart into shreds.

③ Using a slotted spoon remove peppers and onion from cooker. If desired, drizzle meat with some cooking liquid.

④ Spoon some of the meat and vegetables onto one side of each warmed tortilla; top with sour cream. Fold tortilla over filling.

PER SERVING 327 cal, 9 g fat (4 g sat. fat), 37 mg chol, 657 mg sodium, 37 g carb, 4 g fiber, 23 g pro

quick tip To warm tortillas, preheat oven to 350°F. Stack tortillas and wrap tightly in foil. Heat about 10 minutes or until heated through.

Jalapeño Steak 'n' Mushrooms

The tapioca thickens the sauce just enough to coat the meat and mushrooms. Crush the tapioca pearls on a plate with the back of a spoon before combining it with the other ingredients.

MAKES 6 servings **PREP** 25 minutes
COOK 9 hours (low) or 4½ hours (high)

2½ pounds boneless beef chuck steak, cut 1 inch thick

¼ cup packed brown sugar

¼ cup reduced-sodium soy sauce

¼ cup Worcestershire sauce

2 fresh jalapeños, thinly sliced (see note, page 47)

2 tablespoons red wine vinegar

1 tablespoon quick-cooking tapioca, crushed

4 cloves garlic, thinly sliced

1 cup snipped fresh cilantro

2 to 4 3½-inch-diameter portobello mushrooms, stemmed, gills removed from caps, and caps cut into ½-inch-thick slices

1 medium onion, thinly sliced

Fresh cilantro, snipped (optional)

Hot cooked polenta, mashed potatoes, or mashed sweet potatoes (optional)

① Trim fat from meat. Cut meat into 6 serving-size pieces. Place meat in a 3½- or 4-quart slow cooker. For sauce, in a medium bowl combine brown sugar, soy sauce, Worcestershire sauce, jalapeño peppers, vinegar, crushed tapioca, and garlic. Stir in cilantro. Pour sauce over meat in cooker. Top with mushrooms and onion.

② Cover and cook on low-heat setting for 9 to 10 hours or on high-heat setting for 4½ to 5 hours or until meat is tender. If desired, serve with hot cooked polenta and sprinkle with snipped cilantro.

PER SERVING 339 cal, 12 g fat (4 g sat. fat), 108 mg chol, 618 mg sodium, 16 g carb, 1 g fiber, 40 g pro

Jalapeño Steak 'n' Mushrooms

Garlic-Braised Brisket

Garlic-Braised Brisket

If you like garlic, you will love this super-garlicky brisket (30 cloves!). The intensity of the garlic mellows as it cooks, but it still offers plenty of piquant flavor.

MAKES 8 servings **PREP** 45 minutes
COOK 8 hours (low) or 4 hours (high)
STAND 15 minutes **BROIL** 1 minute

1	4- to 5-pound beef brisket
2	medium onions, thinly sliced
1½	cups chicken broth
30	cloves garlic, peeled
2	tablespoons balsamic vinegar
1	teaspoon dried rosemary, crushed
1	teaspoon cracked black pepper
½	teaspoon salt
½	teaspoon dried basil, crushed
2	baguette-style French bread
¼	cup butter, melted
1	recipe Gremolata

① Trim fat from meat; cut meat in half crosswise. Place meat in a 3½- or 4-quart slow cooker. Arrange onions evenly on meat. Add broth, garlic, vinegar, rosemary, pepper, salt, and basil to cooker.

② Cover and cook on low-heat setting for 8 to 9 hours or on high-heat setting for 4 to 4½ hours. Transfer meat to a cutting board; let stand for 15 minutes. When meat is cool enough to handle, slice it thinly across the grain. Use a slotted spoon to remove onions and garlic from slow cooker; set aside. Set aside cooking liquid.

③ While brisket cools, preheat broiler. Cut each loaf of bread in half lengthwise and crosswise to make 8 sandwich rolls. Brush the cut sides of bread with butter. Arrange bread, buttered sides up, on a baking sheet. Broil 4 to 5 inches from the heat for 1 to 2 minutes or until light brown.

④ To serve, arrange brisket slices on roll bottoms. Top with onions and garlic; drizzle with cooking liquid. Sprinkle with Gremolata. Cover with roll tops.

Gremolata: In a small bowl combine ¼ cup chopped fresh parsley, 2 teaspoons finely shredded lemon peel, and 3 cloves garlic, minced. Toss lightly to combine.

PER SERVING 903 cal, 42 g fat (17 g sat. fat), 159 mg chol, 1,191 mg sodium, 72 g carb, 4 g fiber, 57 g pro

Beer-Braised Beef Short Ribs 🍲

These hearty slow-cooked ribs hit the spot on a cold winter night. For the most intense flavor, use a stout, such as Guinness.

MAKES 4 to 6 servings **PREP** 20 minutes
COOK 11 hours (low) or 5½ hours (high)

5	pounds beef short ribs
1	14.5-ounce can beef broth
1	12-ounce can dark beer
1	medium onion, cut into thin wedges
¼	cup molasses
2	tablespoons balsamic vinegar
1	teaspoon dried thyme, crushed
1	teaspoon bottled hot pepper sauce
½	teaspoon salt
	Mashed potatoes or hot buttered noodles (optional)
	Fresh thyme leaves (optional)

① Place ribs in a 5- to 6-quart slow cooker. Add broth, beer, onion, molasses, vinegar, dried thyme, hot pepper sauce, and salt.

② Cover and cook on low-heat setting for 11 to 12 hours or on high-heat setting for 5½ to 6 hours.

③ Using a slotted spoon, transfer ribs to a platter; cover to keep warm. Skim fat from cooking liquid. If desired, serve cooking liquid with ribs and mashed potatoes. If desired, garnish potatoes with fresh thyme leaves.

PER SERVING 481 cal, 19 g fat (8 g sat. fat), 132 mg chol, 821 mg sodium, 22 g carb, 0 g fiber, 46 g pro

Beer-Braised
Beef Short Ribs

Pot Roast Paprikash

Round out this Hungarian-style meal with steamed green beans or sweet peas.

MAKES 8 servings **PREP** 25 minutes
COOK 10 hours (low) or 5 hours + 30 minutes (high)

- 1 2½-pound beef rump roast
- 2 tablespoons paprika
- ½ teaspoon smoked paprika
- 1 14.5-ounce can diced tomatoes, undrained
- 1 14.5-ounce can beef broth
- 3 medium onions, halved and cut into ½-inch slices
- 3 large carrots, coarsely chopped
- 1 12-ounce jar roasted red sweet peppers, drained and cut into ½-inch-wide strips
- ¼ cup water
- 2 tablespoons cornstarch
- 1 8-ounce carton sour cream
   Salt
   Ground black pepper
- 4 ounces dried medium noodles
- ¼ cup butter
- ⅓ cup snipped fresh parsley

① Trim fat from meat; cut meat into 4 pieces. Place meat in a 4- to 5-quart slow cooker. In a small bowl combine paprika and smoked paprika. Sprinkle paprika mixture on beef. Top with tomatoes, broth, onions, carrots, and sweet peppers.

② Cover and cook on low-heat setting for 10 to 12 hours or on high-heat setting for 5 to 6 hours.

③ Using tongs, transfer meat to a cutting board. Use two forks to pull meat apart into coarse shreds. Skim fat from cooking liquid. Stir meat into liquid in cooker. Set cooker on high-heat setting. In a small bowl whisk together the water and cornstarch. Stir into liquid in cooker. Cover and cook for 30 minutes. Stir in sour cream. Season to taste with salt and black pepper.

④ Meanwhile, cook noodles according to package directions; drain. Toss with butter. Serve shredded roast over noodles. Sprinkle with parsley.

PER SERVING 523 cal, 28 g fat (13 g sat. fat), 136 mg chol, 590 mg sodium, 35 g carb, 4 g fiber, 34 g pro

Sloppy Joes with a Kick

The kick in this saucy loose-meat sandwich filling comes from jalapeños (but only if you like it that way).

MAKES 8 servings **PREP** 20 minutes
COOK 6 hours (low) or 3 hours (high)

- 1½ pounds lean ground beef
- 1 cup chopped onion
- 1 clove garlic, minced
- 1 5.5-ounce can vegetable juice
- ½ cup ketchup
- ½ cup water
- 2 tablespoons sugar
- 2 tablespoons chopped, canned jalapeño peppers (see note, page 47) (optional)
- 1 tablespoon prepared mustard
- 2 teaspoons chili powder
- 1 teaspoon Worcestershire sauce
- 8 whole wheat hamburger buns, split and toasted
- ½ cup shredded reduced-fat cheddar cheese (optional)
   Sweet pepper strips (optional)

① In a large skillet cook ground beef, onion, and garlic until meat is brown and onion is tender. Drain off fat.

② Meanwhile, in a 3½- or 4-quart slow cooker combine vegetable juice, ketchup, the water, sugar, jalapeño peppers (if desired), mustard, chili powder, and Worcestershire sauce. Stir in meat mixture.

③ Cover and cook on low-heat setting for 6 to 8 hours or on high-heat setting for 3 to 4 hours. Spoon about ½ cup sandwich filling on each bun bottom. If desired, sprinkle with cheese and serve with sweet pepper strips. Replace bun tops.

PER SERVING 303 cal, 10 g fat (3 g sat. fat), 55 mg chol, 523 mg sodium, 31 g carb, 3 g fiber, 22 g pro

Pot Roast Paprikash

Beef and Carrot Ragu

Beef and Carrot Ragu

Serve this meaty Italian-style sauce over pasta—preferably a hearty type such as rigatoni, pappardelle, or malfada.

MAKES 4 servings **PREP** 25 minutes
COOK 6 hours (low) or 3 hours (high)

- 1 to 1½ pounds boneless beef short ribs
  Salt and black pepper
- 10 cloves garlic
- 8 ounces package peeled fresh baby carrots, chopped
- 1 pound plum tomatoes, chopped
- ½ 6-ounce can tomato paste with basil, garlic, and oregano
- ½ cup water or red wine
  Hot cooked pasta (optional)
  Fresh basil leaves (optional)

① Trim excess fat from rib meat. Cut beef in chunks, then sprinkle lightly with salt and pepper. Place beef in a 3½- or 4-quart slow cooker.

② Smash garlic cloves with the flat side of a chef's knife or meat mallet. Separate and discard garlic skins. Place smashed garlic on beef. Add carrots and tomatoes to slow cooker.

③ In a medium bowl whisk together tomato paste and the water. Poor over meat and vegetables. Cover and cook on low heat setting for for 6 to 8 hours or on high heat setting for 3 to 4 hours.

④ Stir well before serving. If desired, spoon onto hot cooked pasta and sprinkle with basil leaves.

PER SERVING 509 cal, 42 g fat (18 g sat. fat), 86 mg chol, 568 mg sodium, 15 g carb, 4 g fiber, 19 g pro

Lemony Lamb Pitas

Yogurt sauce offers a refreshing tang and crunch (from chopped cucumber) to these rich-tasting, meaty sandwiches.

MAKES 8 servings **PREP** 30 minutes
COOK 8 hours (low) or 4 hours (high)

- 1 large onion, sliced
- 1 2-pound boneless lamb leg roast
- ½ teaspoon lemon-pepper seasoning
- ½ teaspoon dry mustard
- ½ cup chicken broth
- ¼ teaspoon finely shredded lemon peel
- 1 tablespoon lemon juice
- 1 teaspoon snipped fresh rosemary or ¼ teaspoon dried rosemary, crushed
- 2 cloves garlic, minced
- 4 large whole wheat pita bread rounds, halved crosswise
- 8 lettuce leaves
- 1 recipe Yogurt Sauce
- 1 small tomato, seeded and chopped

① Place onion in a 3½- or 4-quart slow cooker. Trim fat from roast. In a small bowl combine lemon-pepper seasoning and dry mustard. Sprinkle evenly on the roast; rub in lightly with your fingers. Place roast in cooker. In a small bowl combine broth, lemon peel, lemon juice, rosemary, and garlic. Pour over all in cooker.

② Cover and cook on low-heat setting for 8 to 10 hours or on high-heat setting for 4 to 5 hours.

③ Remove meat from cooker. Using two forks, shred meat; discard fat. Place meat in a medium bowl. Using a slotted spoon, remove onion from cooker and stir into meat mixture. Discard cooking liquid in cooker.

④ To serve, open pita bread halves to form pockets. Place a lettuce leaf in each pita half. Spoon meat into pita halves. Top with Yogurt Sauce and chopped tomato.

Yogurt Sauce: In a small bowl stir together ½ cup plain low-fat yogurt, ¼ cup chopped and seeded cucumber, and ½ teaspoon lemon-pepper seasoning. Makes about ½ cup.

PER SERVING 293 cal, 7 g fat (2 g sat. fat), 76 mg chol, 515 mg sodium, 28 g carb, 4 g fiber, 29 g pro

Slow-Braised Lamb Shoulder Chops with Sherry Sauce

An immersion blender (sometimes called a stick blender) makes pureeing sauces like the one in this dish—as well as soups—easy, neat, and safe.

MAKES 6 servings **PREP** 20 minutes
COOK 5 hours (low) or 2½ hours (high)

- 1 **cup chopped onion (1 large)**
- ½ **cup chopped carrot (1 medium)**
- 2 **cloves garlic, minced**
- 1 **tablespoon olive oil**
- 6 **lamb shoulder chops, about ¾ inch thick (8 ounces each)**
- 1 **cup reduced-sodium chicken broth**
- ¼ **cup dry sherry**
- 2 **bay leaves**
- ½ **teaspoon salt**
- ¼ **teaspoon cracked black pepper**
- ⅛ **teaspoon ground cloves**

① In a 4- to 5-quart slow cooker combine onion, carrot, and garlic.

② In an extra-large skillet heat oil over medium-high heat. Add lamb chops, half at a time, to skillet; cook chops until brown on both sides. Place chops in slow cooker. Add broth, sherry, bay leaves, salt, pepper, and cloves.

③ Cover and cook on low-heat setting for 5 to 6 hours or on high-heat setting for 2½ to 3 hours. Transfer chops to a serving platter; cover with foil to keep warm.

④ For sauce, discard bay leaves from cooking liquid in slow cooker. Transfer vegetables and cooking liquid to a 4-cup glass measure; skim off fat. Using an immersion blender, process vegetables and cooking liquid until smooth. (Or cool slightly; place in a blender. Cover and blend until smooth.)

⑤ To serve, ladle some sauce on each serving plate. Place a chop on sauce.

PER SERVING 435 cal, 31 g fat (12 g sat. fat), 117 mg chol, 404 mg sodium, 5 g carb, 1 g fiber, 30 g pro

Walnut-Cheese Risotto

Unlike traditional stove-top risotto, there's no stirring to make this creamy (and meatless) rice dish.

MAKES 8 servings **PREP** 20 minutes
COOK 5 hours (low) **STAND** 15 minutes

Nonstick cooking spray
- 1½ **cups converted rice (do not substitute long grain rice)**
- 2 **14-ounce cans vegetable broth**
- 1½ **cups milk**
- 2 **cups shredded carrot**
- 1 **10¾-ounce can condensed cream of mushroom soup**
- 1 **onion, chopped**
- 1 **teaspoon finely shredded lemon peel**
- ¼ **teaspoon black pepper**
- 6 **ounces process Swiss cheese, torn**
- 1 **cup finely shredded Asiago cheese (4 ounces)**
- 1 **cup loose-pack frozen peas**
- ¾ **cup chopped walnuts, toasted**

① Coat a 4- to 5-quart slow cooker with cooking spray. Add rice, broth, milk, carrots, mushroom soup, onion, lemon peel, and pepper to prepared cooker; stir lightly to combine. Cover and cook on low-heat setting for 5 to 5½ hours.

② Stir in Swiss cheese, Asiago cheese, peas, and walnuts. Remove liner from cooker, if possible, or turn off cooker. Let stand, covered, for 15 minutes before serving.

PER SERVING 428 cal, 21 g fat (9 g sat. fat), 38 mg chol, 1,163 mg sodium, 43 g carb, 3 g fiber, 17 g pro

Slow-Braised Lamb Shoulder
Chops with Sherry

Crustless Spinach
and Mushroom Quiche

Crustless Spinach and Mushroom Quiche

Perfect for Sunday brunch, this slow-cooker quiche cooks while you're at church or doing the morning-paper crossword puzzle—and it's ready when you are.

MAKES 6 to 8 servings **PREP** 20 minutes
COOK 4 hours (low) or 2 hours (high) **COOL** 15 minutes

	Disposable slow cooker liner
	Nonstick cooking spray
1	10-ounce package frozen chopped spinach, thawed and well drained
4	slices bacon
1	tablespoon olive oil
2	cups coarsely chopped portobello mushrooms
½	cup chopped red sweet pepper (1 small)
1½	cups shredded Gruyère or Swiss cheese (6 ounces)
8	eggs
2	cups half-and-half or whole milk
2	tablespoons snipped fresh chives
½	teaspoon salt
¼	teaspoon black pepper
½	cup packaged biscuit mix

① Line a 3½- or 4-quart slow cooker with a disposable slow cooker liner; coat liner with cooking spray. Using clean paper towels, press spinach to remove as much liquid as possible; set aside.

② In a medium skillet cook bacon until crisp; drain, crumble, and set aside. Discard drippings. In the same skillet heat oil over medium heat. Add mushrooms and sweet pepper; cook and stir until tender. Stir in spinach and cheese.

③ In a medium bowl combine eggs, half-and-half, chives, salt, and black pepper. Stir egg mixture into spinach mixture in skillet. Gently fold in biscuit mix. Pour into prepared slow cooker. Sprinkle with bacon.

④ Cover and cook on low-heat setting for 4 to 5 hours or on high-heat setting for 2 to 2½ hours or until a knife inserted into the center comes out clean. Turn off cooker. If possible, remove crockery liner from cooker. Cool for 15 to 30 minutes before serving.

PER SERVING 431 cal, 31 g fat (15 g sat. fat), 349 mg chol, 699 mg sodium, 15 g carb, 2 g fiber, 25 g pro

Cajun Seasoned Vegetarian Gumbo

Okra contains a natural thickening agent that gives this vegetarian version of the New Orleans classic body and texture.

MAKES 6 servings **PREP** 10 minutes
COOK 6 hours (low) or 3 hours (high)

2	15-ounce cans black beans, rinsed and drained
1	28-ounce can diced tomatoes, undrained
1	16-ounce package frozen sweet pepper and onion stir-fry vegetables
2	cups frozen cut okra
2	to 3 teaspoons Cajun seasoning
3	cups hot cooked white or brown rice
	Chopped green onions (optional)

① In a 3½- to 4½-quart slow cooker combine beans, tomatoes, frozen stir-fry vegetables, frozen okra, and Cajun seasoning.

② Cover and cook on low-heat setting for 6 to 8 hours or on high-heat setting for 3 to 4 hours.

③ Serve gumbo in shallow bowls over hot cooked rice. If desired, sprinkle with green onions.

PER SERVING 250 cal, 1 g fat (0 g sat. fat), 0 mg chol, 675 mg sodium, 52 g carb, 10 g fiber, 14 g pro

Cajun Seasoned Vegetarian Gumbo

For meals with universal appeal, turn to hearty sandwiches and pizzas. The possibilities for these family favorites are nearly endless—just pile on a new ingredient or try a different bread or spread.

252   259   260

SANDWICHES & PIZZAS

267

Open-Face Chicken Salad Sandwiches

Substitute thin slices of smoked Gouda cheese for the provolone, if you prefer.

MAKES 4 sandwiches **START TO FINISH** 25 minutes

- 2 tablespoons olive oil
- 14 ounces chicken tenders
- 2 cups seedless red grapes, whole and or/halved
  Salt and freshly ground black pepper
- 6 cups fresh baby spinach
- 2 tablespoons red wine vinegar
- 1 baguette-style French bread
- 4 ounces provolone cheese, thinly sliced

① Preheat broiler. Line a 15 x 10 x 1-inch baking pan with foil; lightly brush with some olive oil. Place chicken and grapes in a single layer in pan; drizzle remaining oil, then lightly sprinkle with salt and pepper. Broil, 2 to 3 inches from heat, for 10 minutes or until chicken is cooked through and begins to brown.

② For chicken salad, in a large bowl toss together spinach, cooked chicken, grapes, any pan juices, and vinegar.

③ Cut baguette in 4 portions, slice nearly through, place open on baking sheet, then top with cheese. Broil 2 to 3 minutes to melt cheese. Layer salad on baguettes. Drizzle with any remaining dressing in bowl. Top with freshly ground black pepper.

PER SANDWICH 822 cal, 32 g fat (10 g sat. fat), 60 mg chol, 1,646 mg sodium, 96 g carb, 7 g fiber, 38 g pro

Open-Face Chicken Salad Sandwiches

Chicken, Kraut, and Apple Panini ♥

Tart Granny Smith apples are a good choice for making these sauerkraut-stuffed sandwiches.

MAKES 4 panini **PREP** 15 minutes **COOK** 12 minutes

- 1 cup canned sauerkraut
- 8 slices very thinly sliced firm-texture whole wheat bread
  Nonstick cooking spray
- 12 ounces cooked, sliced chicken breast
- 1 apple, cored and thinly sliced
- 4 thin slices reduced-fat Swiss cheese (2 to 3 ounces total)

① Place sauerkraut in a colander and rinse with cold water. Drain well, using a spoon to press out excess liquid. Set aside.

② Lightly coat 1 side of each bread slice with cooking spray. Place 4 bread slices, coated sides down, on a work surface. Top with chicken, sauerkraut, apple slices, and cheese. Top with the remaining 4 bread slices, coated sides up.

③ Coat an unheated grill pan, large skillet, or panini press with cooking spray. Preheat over medium-low heat for 1 to 2 minutes. Add sandwiches, in batches if necessary. Place a heavy skillet on sandwiches in skillet. Cook over medium-low heat for 6 to 8 minutes or until toasted. Using hot pads, carefully remove top skillet. Turn sandwiches; top with skillet and cook for 6 to 8 minutes or until bottoms are toasted.

PER PANINI 283 cal, 7 g fat (3 g sat. fat), 79 mg chol, 457 mg sodium, 21 g carb, 4 g fiber, 34 g pro

quick tip Having cooked chicken breast on hand for making sandwiches or tossing onto greens for a quick main-dish salad is a smart idea. The best way to cook chicken for future use is poaching, which helps prevent the meat from drying out. Place boneless, skinless chicken breasts in a large skillet. Add 1 to 2 cups water. Bring water to boiling; reduce heat, cover, and cook for 9 to 14 minutes or until chicken reaches 160°F. Cool, then refrigerate in a tightly sealed container for 3 to 4 days.

Indian-Spiced Chicken Pitas

Indian-Spiced Chicken Pitas ♥

Marinating chicken in yogurt—as is traditional in recipes for tandoori chicken—keeps it moist, gives it flavor, and tenderizes it.

MAKES 4 pitas **START TO FINISH** 30 minutes

- 1 cup plain fat-free yogurt
- 1 teaspoon garam masala
- ½ teaspoon bottled hot pepper sauce
- ¼ teaspoon salt
- 12 ounces skinless, boneless chicken breast halves, cut into bite-size strips
  Nonstick cooking spray
- 2 whole wheat pita bread rounds, halved crosswise
- 1 cup refrigerated mango and papaya slices, drained and coarsely chopped
- 1 tablespoon tiny fresh mint leaves

① In a small bowl combine yogurt, garam masala, hot pepper sauce, and salt. Pour three-fourths of the marinade into a resealable plastic bag; refrigerate the remaining marinade until serving time. Add chicken to marinade in plastic bag. Seal bag; turn to coat chicken. Marinate in the refrigerator for 15 minutes. Drain chicken, discarding marinade.

② Coat an large unheated nonstick skillet with cooking spray. Heat skillet over medium heat. Add chicken to hot skillet; cook about 5 minutes or until tender and no longer pink, turning once.

③ To serve, divide chicken evenly among pita bread halves. Drizzle with reserved marinade. Top with chopped fruit; sprinkle with fresh mint.

PER PITA 249 cal, 2 g fat (0 g sat. fat), 51 mg chol, 430 mg sodium, 32 g carb, 3 g fiber, 26 g pro

Chicken Lettuce Wraps

Butterhead or Bibb lettuce is especially tender and sweet—a good choice for these low-carb wraps.

MAKES 4 servings **START TO FINISH** 20 minutes

- 2 6-ounce packages refrigerated cooked chicken breast strips
- 2 cups shredded cabbage with carrot (coleslaw mix)
- 1 medium red sweet pepper, cut into strips
- 2 green onions, cut up
- 2 tablespoons snipped fresh cilantro
- 2 tablespoons teriyaki sauce or ⅓ cup bottled Thai peanut sauce
- 8 leaves butterhead (Bibb) or green leaf lettuce

① In a large skillet cook and stir chicken breast strips over medium heat until heated through; set aside.

② In a food processor combine coleslaw mix, red pepper, green onions, and cilantro; cover and process with several on/off turns until finely chopped.

③ Transfer slaw mixture and teriyaki sauce to the skillet with chicken. Cook and stir over medium heat until heated through Spoon onto lettuce leaves; roll up.

PER SERVING 131 cal, 2 g fat (1 g sat. fat), 55 mg chol, 748 mg sodium, 9 g carb, 2 g fiber, 21 g pro

Sandwiches aren't just for lunch. Hearty fillings, veggies, and flavorful sauces make them supper-ready too.

Peanut-Ginger Lettuce Wraps 🍲 ♥

If you don't have leftover cooked chicken, it's easy to quickly cook some. See the Quick Tip on page 244 for directions.

MAKES 4 servings **START TO FINISH** 20 minutes

- 2 cups chopped, cooked chicken breast
- 2 cups shredded cabbage with carrot (coleslaw mix)
- ½ cup chopped carrot (1 medium)
- ¼ cup chopped green onions (2)
- 2 tablespoons unsalted peanuts
- 1 teaspoon minced fresh ginger
- ⅓ cup bottled light Asian salad dressing
- ⅓ cup drained canned crushed pineapple
- 12 lettuce leaves (Boston, bibb, or green leaf)

① In a food processor, half at a time, combine the chicken, coleslaw mix, carrot, green onions, peanuts, and ginger; cover and process with several on/off turns until finely chopped. Transfer to a large bowl. Add salad dressing and pineapple to salad; stir to combine well.

② Spoon about ¼ cup salad onto each lettuce leaf; roll up.

PER SERVINGS 221 cal, 8 g fat (2 g sat. fat), 60 mg chol, 267 mg sodium, 12 g carb, 2 g fiber, 24 g pro

Mediterranean Chicken Pita Sandwiches ♥

The chicken, chickpea, and veggie filling makes a nice salad on its own, without the pita bread. If you'd like to serve it that way, cut the cucumber in small dice and stir it in rather than slicing it and layering it on a sandwich.

MAKES 4 sandwiches **START TO FINISH** 25 minutes

- 1 cup chopped cooked chicken breast
- ½ of a 15-ounce can garbanzo beans (chickpeas), rinsed and drained (about ¾ cup)
- ½ cup diced tomato
- ¼ cup thinly sliced red onion
- ¼ cup crumbled reduced-fat feta cheese
- ⅓ cup plain low-fat yogurt
- 1 tablespoon snipped fresh mint
- 1 clove garlic, minced
- ¼ teaspoon ground cumin
- ¼ teaspoon cracked black pepper
- ⅛ teaspoon salt
- 2 large whole wheat pita bread rounds
- ½ of a medium cucumber, thinly sliced

① For filling, in a large bowl toss together chicken, garbanzo beans, diced tomato, red onion, and feta cheese. For dressing, in a small bowl combine yogurt, mint, garlic, cumin, black pepper, and salt. Spoon dressing on filling; toss to evenly combine.

② To serve, spoon filling on 1 pita bread round. Top with cucumber slices and a second pita bread round. Cut into 4 wedges to serve.

PER SANDWICH 242 cal, 4 g fat (1 g sat. fat), 33 mg chol, 416 mg sodium, 32 g carb, 5 g fiber, 20 g pro

Peanut-Ginger Lettuce Wraps

Bacon-Tomato Melts

Bacon-Tomato Melts

This open-face twist on the classic BLT is best in summer, at the peak of tomato season.

MAKES 4 sandwiches **PREP** 25 minutes **BROIL** 3 minutes

 2 large tomatoes
 ¼ cup light sour cream
 1 green onion, thinly sliced
 1 clove garlic, minced
 ⅛ teaspoon cayenne pepper or ¼ teaspoon paprika
 ⅛ teaspoon ground cumin
 4 ½-inch slices bakery-style or sandwich-style whole wheat bread
 2 cups fresh spinach leaves
 8 slices turkey bacon, cooked according to package directions
 ½ cup shredded reduced-fat Mexican-style cheese blend (2 ounces)

① Preheat broiler. Slice tomatoes. Seed and chop 1 or 2 slices to equal ¼ cup chopped tomato. Set remaining tomato slices aside. In a small bowl combine the ¼ cup chopped tomato, the sour cream, green onion, garlic, cayenne pepper, and cumin. Set aside.

② Place bread slices on a baking sheet. Broil 4 to 5 inches from the heat for 2 to 3 minutes or until toasted, turning once. If desired, set aside some of the spinach leaves for garnish. Top bread with the remaining spinach leaves, tomato slices, sour cream mixture, and bacon. If desired, top with reserved spinach leaves. Add cheese. Broil for 1 to 2 minutes more or until cheese is melted.

PER SANDWICH 206 cal, 10 g fat (5 g sat. fat), 42 mg chol, 623 mg sodium, 15 g carb, 3 g fiber, 12 g pro

Super Sub 🍲

This crusty ham, salami, and cheese sandwich is perfect picnic fare. Just wait to attach the peppers to the sandwich tops—and wrap the sandwiches tightly in foil before placing in a cooler.

MAKES 6 sandwiches **START TO FINISH** 20 minutes

 1 baguette-style whole grain or regular French bread, split in half horizontally
 ¼ cup bottled Italian salad dressing
 4 green lettuce leaves
 6 ounces thinly sliced cooked ham
 6 ounces sliced salami
 6 slices Swiss or provolone cheese
 3 thin slices red onion, separated into rings (optional)
 1 tomato, thinly sliced
 6 sweet cherry peppers

① Lay bread on a work surface, cut sides up. Drizzle cut sides of bread with salad dressing. Arrange lettuce leaves on bottom half, tearing to fit. Layer ham, salami, and Swiss cheese on lettuce. Top with onion rings, if desired, and tomato slices. Add top half of bread. Attach peppers to the top of the loaf with decorative sandwich picks. Cut into 6 portions.

PER SANDWICH 503 cal, 21 g fat (9 g sat. fat), 66 mg chol, 1,620 mg sodium, 49 g carb, 3 g fiber, 32 g pro

Super Sub

Sloppy Joes 🍲

Sloppy Joes of any kind are popular with kids, but the pizza variation—studded with pepperoni and topped with melty mozzarella cheese—is a can't-miss proposition.

MAKES 6 sandwiches **START TO FINISH** 25 minutes

- 1 pound lean ground beef or ground pork
- ½ cup chopped onion (1 medium)
- ½ cup chopped green and/or yellow sweet pepper (1 small)
- 1 8-ounce can tomato sauce
- 2 tablespoons water
- 1 to 1½ teaspoons chili powder
- 1 teaspoon Worcestershire sauce
- ½ teaspoon garlic salt
  Dash of bottled hot pepper sauce
- 6 kaiser rolls or hamburger buns, split and toasted

① In a large skillet cook beef, onion, and sweet pepper until meat is brown and vegetables are tender, stirring to break up any meat. Drain off fat.

② Stir tomato sauce, the water, chili powder, Worcestershire sauce, garlic salt, and hot pepper sauce into beef mixture in skillet. Bring to boiling; reduce heat. Simmer, uncovered, for 5 minutes, stirring occasionally. Serve on rolls.

PER SANDWICH 311 cal, 10 g fat (3 g sat. fat), 48 mg chol, 632 mg sodium, 35 g carb, 2 g fiber, 20 g pro

Pizza Joes: Prepare as above, except substitute one 14-ounce jar pizza sauce for the tomato sauce, water, chili powder, Worcestershire sauce, garlic salt, and hot pepper sauce. Add ½ cup chopped pepperoni. Serve on toasted rolls with slices of mozzarella cheese.

Beef and Tapenade Focaccia Sandwiches 🍲

Tapenade is a French condiment made from olives, capers, garlic, olive oil, lemon juice, seasonings, and anchovies. The thick paste is spread on bread or served with crudités, grilled fish, or meat.

MAKES 6 sandwiches **START TO FINISH** 15 minutes

- 1 10-inch round or square focaccia
- ½ of a 8-ounce tub cream cheese spread with chive and onion
- ½ cup purchased black olive tapenade
- 1 pound thinly sliced deli roast beef or turkey
- 2 tomatoes, thinly sliced
- 2 romaine leaves

① Cut focaccia in half horizontally. Spread bottom half with cream cheese, then with tapenade. Top with roast beef, tomatoes, and romaine leaves. Add top half of focaccia.

② Cut into 6 wedges or rectangles. Secure portions with wooden skewers.

PER SANDWICH 467 cal, 23 g fat (8 g sat. fat), 53 mg chol, 1,450 mg sodium, 37 g carb, 4 g fiber, 23 g pro

> ❮ Delicious condiments—tapenade, mustard, flavored mayo—turns a simple sandwich into something special. ❯

Gyro Sandwiches

Gyros

This Greek-style sandwich made with ground lamb and generous seasoning comes as close to the restaurant version as possible.

MAKES 4 sandwiches **PREP** 20 minutes **BROIL** 10 minutes

- 1 pound ground lamb or beef
- 2 teaspoons dried minced onion
- 1 teaspoon garlic powder
- 1 teaspoon Greek seasoning or dried oregano, crushed
- ½ teaspoon salt
- ¼ teaspoon black pepper
- 1 6-ounce container plain low-fat yogurt or ⅔ cup sour cream
- ¼ cup chopped, seeded cucumber
- 2 teaspoons snipped fresh mint or parsley
- 1 clove garlic, minced
- 4 soft pita bread rounds, warmed (see Quick Tip, below)
- 1 medium tomato, thinly sliced
- ¼ cup thinly slivered red onion
- ⅓ cup crumbled feta cheese

① Preheat broiler. In a medium bowl combine lamb, minced onion, garlic powder, Greek seasoning, salt, and pepper. Shape meat into four ½-inch-thick oval patties. Place patties on the unheated rack of a broiler pan.

② Broil patties 4 to 5 inches from heat for 10 to 12 minutes or until meat is no longer pink and juices run clear (160°F.), turning patties once.

③ Meanwhile, in a small bowl stir together yogurt, cucumber, mint, and garlic; set aside.

④ To serve, layer pitas with tomato slices, yogurt sauce, red onion, feta cheese, and lamb patties; fold over.

PER SANDWICH 462 cal, 20 g fat (9 g sat. fat); 89 mg chol, 868 mg sodium, 41 g carb, 2 g fiber, 29 g pro

quick tip To warm pitas, wrap in microwave-safe paper towels. Microwave on high for 1 minute or until warm.

Tuna Club Sandwiches with Roasted Pepper Sauce

Serve this towering sandwich with a knife and fork.

MAKES 4 sandwiches **START TO FINISH** 25 minutes

- ⅓ cup bottled ranch salad dressing
- ½ cup bottled roasted red sweet peppers, drained
- 1 12-ounce can solid white tuna, drained and broken in chunks
- 1 8.75-ounce can whole kernel corn, drained
- 12 extra-thin slices sandwich bread, toasted
  Butterhead lettuce leaves (optional)

① For the roasted red pepper sauce, in a blender container combine salad dressing and half the roasted red sweet peppers; process until nearly smooth.

② For tuna filling, chop remaining peppers. In a bowl combine chopped peppers with tuna, corn, and ¼ cup of the roasted red pepper sauce.

③ For each club sandwich, spread 2 slices of toasted bread with tuna filling, layer with lettuce leaves (if desired), stack the 2 slices, then top with a third slice of toast. Cut in half diagonally. Serve with remaining roasted red pepper sauce.

PER SANDWICH 441 cal, 17 g fat (2 g sat. fat); 41 mg chol, 1,020 mg sodium, 47 g carb, 1 g fiber, 29 g pro

Tuna Club Sandwiches with Roasted Pepper Sauce

Asian Tuna Wraps

To shred the bok choy, simply cut it in very thin slices with a sharp chef's knife.

MAKES 4 wraps **PREP** 15 minutes

- 2 6-ounce cans very low-sodium solid white tuna (water pack), drained and broken into chunks
- 3 tablespoons bottled sesame-ginger salad dressing
- ¼ cup light mayonnaise
- 1 teaspoon minced garlic
- ½ teaspoon minced fresh ginger
- 4 8-inch low-carb whole wheat flour tortillas or regular whole wheat tortillas
- 2 cups shredded bok choy
- 1 medium red sweet pepper, thinly sliced
- ½ cup jicama, cut into matchstick-size pieces

① In a large bowl stir together tuna, salad dressing, 2 tablespoons of the mayonnaise, the garlic, and ginger. Spread remaining 2 tablespoons mayonnaise on 1 side of each tortilla. Divide bok choy, red pepper, and jicama among wraps. Top with tuna and roll up.

PER WRAP 282 cal, 11 g fat (1 g sat. fat), 43 mg chol, 549 mg sodium, 20 g carb, 10 g fiber, 24 g pro

quick tip If you have a microplane, use it to mince the fresh ginger. Peel the ginger, then rub it on the rough side of the grater.

Tuna and Hummus Wrap

To seed a cucumber peel it, cut it in half horizontally, and then use the tip of a small spoon to scrape the seeds out of each half.

MAKES 4 wraps **START TO FINISH** 20 minutes

- 1 6-ounce can very low sodium chunk white tuna (water pack), drained
- 1 cucumber, peeled, seeded, and finely chopped
- 1 tomato, seeded and chopped
- 2 tablespoons olive oil
- 1 tablespoon snipped fresh dill or 1 teaspoon dried dill, crushed
- ¼ teaspoon black pepper
- 4 whole wheat tortillas
- ⅓ cup refrigerated cucumber-dill hummus
- 4 cups torn packaged lettuce (such as hearts of romaine, European blend, or Mediterranean blend)

① In a medium bowl stir together tuna, cucumber, tomato, oil, dill, and pepper.

② Spread hummus on 1 side of each tortilla. Toss tuna with lettuce. Divide evenly among the tortillas. Roll up.

PER WRAP 280 cal, 11 g fat (1 g sat. fat), 19 mg chol, 482 mg sodium, 32 g carb, 4 g fiber, 16 g pro

Tuna and Hummus Wrap

Egg Salad Sandwiches

Build a Better Pizza

Build a Better Pizza

Adding fresh herbs to the pizza dough infuses it with flavor without adding fat or calories.

MAKES 2 to 4 servings **PREP** 15 minutes
COOK 8 minutes per pizza

- 1 6- to 6.5-ounce package pizza crust mix
- 1 to 2 tablespoons snipped fresh parsley, oregano, and/or basil
- 1 tablespoon olive oil
- ½ cup bottled pasta sauce or marinara sauce
- 8 ounces fresh mozzarella cheese, sliced
- ½ cup Canadian bacon cut into strips, or cooked and chopped or crumbled bacon, ground beef, or Italian sausage
- 1 medium tomato, chopped
- ¼ cup chopped or sliced pitted green olives
   Olive oil and/or cracked black pepper
   Crumbled or finely shredded Parmesan cheese

① Prepare pizza crust mix according to package directions, adding herbs to dry mixture. Divide dough in half. On a lightly floured surface, roll each dough portion into a circle about 9 inches in diameter and ⅛ inch thick.

② Preheat a greased grill pan or griddle over medium heat. For each pizza, place one crust on the pan. Brush dough with some of the 1 tablespoon olive oil. Cook 3 minutes or until golden brown on the bottom. Use a wide spatula to turn crust over. Brush dough with more oil. Cook for 3 minutes more or until bottom is browned. Turn again.

③ Spread crust with half the pasta sauce. Top with half the mozzarella slices. Scatter half the meat, tomato, and olives on cheese. Drizzle with additional olive oil, and sprinkle with black pepper and Parmesan. Cook about 2 minutes or until toppings are heated through. Remove to a serving plate.

PER SERVING 508 cal, 31 g fat (12 g sat. fat),54 mg chol, 1,087 mg sodium, 35 g carb, 1 g fiber, 20 g pro

Spinach Barbecue Chicken Pizza

BBQ chicken pizza—a new American favorite—gets a nutritional boost with chopped spinach.

MAKES 4 servings **PREP** 15 minutes **BAKE** 10 minutes
OVEN 450°F

- 1 12-inch whole wheat thin Italian bread shell (Boboli)
- 1 9-ounce package frozen chopped cooked chicken, thawed
- ½ cup bottled barbecue sauce
- 2 cups packaged fresh baby spinach
- 1 cup shredded reduced-fat Monterey Jack cheese or part-skim mozzarella cheese (4 ounces)
- 2 tablespoons snipped fresh cilantro

① Preheat oven to 450°F. Place bread shell on a large baking sheet. In a medium bowl combine chicken and barbecue sauce. Evenly spread chicken on bread shell. Sprinkle with spinach. Top with cheese.

② Bake for 10 to 12 minutes or until cheese is melted and pizza is heated through. Sprinkle with cilantro.

PER SERVING 385 cal, 13 g fat (5 g sat. fat), 65 mg chol, 1,258 mg sodium, 40 g carb, 6 g fiber, 33 g pro

Spinach Barbecue Chicken Pizza

Hearty Pineapple Pizza

Put on a little Hawaiian music while you make this popular American-style pizza.

MAKES 4 servings **PREP** 15 minutes **BAKE** 8 minutes
OVEN 450°F

- 1 8-ounce can pizza sauce
- 1 12-inch whole wheat thin Italian bread shell (Boboli)
- 1 large green sweet pepper, seeded and thinly sliced
- ½ cup thinly sliced quartered red onion
- 1 8-ounce can crushed pineapple, well drained
- ½ of a 3½-ounce package pizza-style Canadian-style bacon
- ¾ cup shredded part-skim mozzarella cheese (3 ounces)

① Preheat oven to 450°F. Spread pizza sauce on bread shell. Top with sweet pepper, red onion, pineapple, and Canadian-style bacon. Sprinkle with mozzarella cheese. Place pizza on a large baking pan.

② Bake for 8 to 10 minutes or until cheese is melted and pizza is heated through.

PER SERVING 357 cal, 9 g fat (3 g sat. fat), 20 mg chol, 876 mg sodium, 49 g carb, 6 g fiber, 18 g pro

Hearty Pineapple Pizza

Fontina Cheese and Artichoke Pizza

Drizzle wedges of the baked pizza with warmed Alfredo sauce, if you like.

MAKES 6 servings **START TO FINISH** 30 minutes
OVEN 450°F

- 1 medium red onion, thinly sliced
- 2 cloves garlic, minced
- 1 tablespoon olive oil or vegetable oil
- 1 12-inch Italian bread shell (Boboli)
- 1½ cups shredded fontina or Swiss cheese (6 ounces)
- ½ of a 9-ounce package frozen artichokes, thawed and cut up
- ½ cup pitted kalamata olives, halved or quartered

  Coarse ground black pepper

  Alfredo pasta sauce, warmed (optional)

① Preheat oven to 450°F. In a medium skillet cook onion and garlic in hot oil over medium heat until onion is tender and golden brown, stirring occasionally.

② Place bread shell on a lightly greased baking sheet. Bake for 5 minutes. Sprinkle with ½ cup of the cheese. Top with artichokes, olives, and cooked onions. Sprinkle with the remaining 1 cup cheese. Sprinkle lightly with pepper.

③ Bake for 8 to 10 minutes or until heated through and cheese is melted. If desired, serve pizza with warm Alfredo sauce.

PER SERVING 368 cal, 18 g fat (6 g sat. fat), 38 mg chol, 780 mg sodium, 38 g carb, 2 g fiber, 16 g pro

The salads, veggies, and breads that round out a meal usually command less attention than the main dish, but they bring real interest to the table. These creative side dishes are both nutritious and satisfying.

276 288 296

TASTY SIDE DISHES

279

Broccoli Rabe with Garlic ♥

Cook the broccoli rabe the day you buy it. The longer it sits, the more bitter-tasting it can get.

MAKES 12 servings **START TO FINISH** 20 minutes

- 3 pounds broccoli rabe or 7 cups broccoli florets
- 2 tablespoons olive oil
- 6 cloves garlic, minced
- ¼ cup reduced-sodium chicken broth
- ½ teaspoon ground black pepper
- ¼ teaspoon salt

① If using broccoli raab, remove large leaves and, if necessary, cut stems to 6- to 8-inch lengths. In a 6- to 8-quart Dutch oven cook broccoli rabe, half at a time if necessary, in a large amount of boiling water for 3 minutes if using broccoli raab or 6 minutes if using broccoli florets. Drain well; gently squeeze broccoli raab if necessary to dry it thoroughly.

② In the same Dutch oven heat oil over medium heat. Add garlic; cook and stir for 30 seconds. Carefully add drained broccoli rabe (oil will spatter if vegetables are not drained well); cook and stir for 1 minute. Add broth and cook, uncovered, until all the broth has evaporated, stirring frequently. Stir in pepper and salt. Serve immediately.

PER SERVING 48 cal, 3 g fat (0 g sat. fat), 0 mg chol, 98 mg sodium, 4 g carb, 3 g fiber, 4 g pro

Great Greek Green Beans 🍲

Serve these Greek-inspired green beans with grilled chicken or salmon.

MAKES 6 servings **PREP** 10 minutes **COOK** 20 minutes

- ½ cup chopped onion
- 1 clove garlic, minced
- 2 tablespoons olive oil
- 1 28-ounce can diced tomatoes
- ¼ cup sliced pitted ripe olives
- 1 teaspoon dried oregano, crushed
- 2 9-ounce packages or one 16-ounce package frozen French-cut green beans, thawed and drained
- ½ cup crumbled feta cheese (2 ounces)

① In a large skillet cook onion and garlic in hot oil about 5 minutes or until tender. Add undrained tomatoes, olives, and oregano. Bring to boiling; reduce heat. Boil gently, uncovered, for 10 minutes. Add beans. Return to boiling. Boil gently, uncovered, about 8 minutes or until desired consistency and beans are tender.

② Transfer to a serving bowl; sprinkle with cheese. If desired, serve with a slotted spoon.

PER SERVING 132 cal, 7 g fat (2 g sat. fat), 8 mg chol, 419 mg sodium, 15 g carb, 5 g fiber, 4 g pro

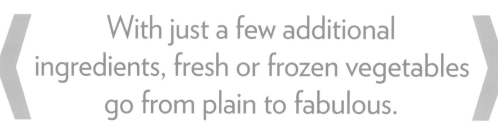

⟨ With just a few additional ingredients, fresh or frozen vegetables go from plain to fabulous. ⟩

Apple-Garlic Loaves

A surprising combination of ingredients—sweet, savory, and tart—top these unusual loaves. Slice them to keep the topping in place.

MAKES 24 slices **PREP** 20 minutes **BAKE** 10 minutes **OVEN** 375°F

- 3 medium Granny Smith apples, cored (about 1 pound)
- 1 tablespoon butter
- 4 large cloves garlic, coarsely chopped
- ½ cup quick-cooking or regular rolled oats
- ½ cup packed brown sugar
- 1 tablespoon lemon juice
- 2 20-ounce loaves purchased ciabatta bread or other crusty bread
- 3 tablespoons butter, melted

① Thinly slice half the apples; coarsely chop remaining apples. In a large skillet melt 1 tablespoon butter. Add apples, garlic, and oats. Cook over medium heat for 5 to 8 minutes or until apples begin to soften, stirring occasionally. Remove from heat; stir in brown sugar and lemon juice. Immediately top bread, or transfer to a medium bowl; cover and chill up to 24 hours.

② Preheat oven to 375°F. Place loaves on a large baking sheet (see quick tip). Brush tops of loaves with melted butter. Spoon half the topping onto each loaf, pressing in slightly. Bake, uncovered, for 10 minutes or until warmed through. Transfer to a cutting surface. Slice carefully to avoid dislodging apples.

PER SLICE 180 cal, 4 g fat (1 g sat. fat), 5 mg chol, 293 mg sodium, 32 g carb, 2 g fiber, 5 g pro

quick tip If the loaves do not have flat tops, slice off the rounded portions to make flat surfaces.

Bacon-Onion Biscuits

A warm, buttery, flaky biscuit—with bacon and onions in it? Need we say more?

PREP 30 minutes **BAKE** 10 minutes **OVEN** 450°F

- 4 slices bacon, chopped
- 1 large onion, chopped
- 3 cups all-purpose flour
- 1 tablespoon baking powder
- 1 tablespoon sugar
- ½ teaspoon salt
- ¾ teaspoon cream of tartar
- ¾ cup butter
- 1 cup milk

① Preheat oven to 450°F. In a skillet cook bacon and onion until bacon is slightly crisp and onion is tender. Drain off and discard fat.

② In a bowl stir together flour, baking powder, sugar, salt, and cream of tartar. Using a pastry blender, cut in butter until mixture resembles coarse crumbs. Make a well in center. Combine milk and bacon mixture; add all at once to flour mixture. Using a fork, stir just until moistened.

③ Turn dough out onto a lightly floured surface. Knead by folding and gently pressing dough for four to six strokes or just until dough holds together. Pat or lightly roll dough to ¾-inch thickness. Cut with a floured 2½-inch biscuit cutter, rerolling scraps as necessary.

④ Place biscuits 1 inch apart on ungreased baking sheet. Bake 10 to 14 minutes or until golden.

PER SERVING 294 cal, 18 g fat (10 g sat. fat), 41 mg chol, 354 mg sodium, 27 g carb, 1 g fiber, 6 g pro

Not every menu requires dessert, but something sweet at the end of a meal makes a delicious finale. Packaged mixes, purchased doughs, and flavor-packed ingredients are the keys to these pleasing treats.

312

318

325

SWEET TOOTH-DESSERTS

305

Zucchini-Banana Snack Cake ♥

This fruit-and-veggie-packed, whole-grain snack cake is a treat you can feel good about serving your family.

MAKES 24 servings **PREP** 20 minutes
BAKE 20 minutes **OVEN** 350°F

Nonstick cooking spray
1 cup all-purpose flour
1 cup whole wheat flour
¼ cup flaxseed meal or wheat germ
¼ cup unsweetened cocoa powder
2 teaspoons baking powder
½ teaspoon salt
½ cup refrigerated or frozen egg product, thawed, or 2 eggs, slightly beaten
¾ cup sugar
½ cup canola oil
⅓ cup fat-free milk
1 cup shredded zucchini, peeled, if desired
1 medium-size ripe banana, mashed (½ cup)
½ cup miniature semisweet chocolate pieces (optional)

① Preheat oven to 350°F. Lightly coat a 13 x 9 x 2-inch baking pan with nonstick cooking spray; set aside. In a large bowl combine all-purpose flour, whole wheat flour, flaxseed meal, cocoa powder, baking powder, and salt. Make a well in center of flour mixture; set aside.

② In a medium bowl whisk together egg, sugar, canola oil, and milk until well mixed. Stir in zucchini and banana. Add zucchini mixture all at once to flour mixture. Stir just until moistened. Fold in chocolate pieces, if desired. Pour batter into prepared pan, spreading evenly.

③ Bake 20 to 25 minutes or until top springs back when lightly touched. Cool completely on a wire rack. Cut into rectangles.

PER SERVING 118 cal, 5 g fat (0 g sat. fat), 0 mg chol, 80 mg sodium, 16 g carb, 1 g fiber, 2 g pro

Apple-Date Cake

Good choices for cooking apples include Granny Smith, Golden Delicious, Jonathan, and McIntosh.

MAKES 12 servings **PREP** 30 minutes
BAKE 25 minutes **OVEN** 350°F

Nonstick cooking spray
⅔ cup fat-free milk
⅔ cup chopped pitted dates
¼ teaspoon salt
¾ cup coarsely shredded peeled cooking apple
1 teaspoon vanilla
1 egg, lightly beaten
2 tablespoons vegetable oil
½ cup chopped pecans
¼ cup packed brown sugar
1 tablespoon butter, softened
1 teaspoon all-purpose flour
1 teaspoon ground cinnamon
1½ cups all-purpose flour
1 teaspoon baking powder
½ teaspoon baking soda

① Preheat oven to 350°F. Lightly coat an 8 x 8 x 2-inch baking pan with cooking spray. Set aside.

② In a small saucepan combine milk, dates, and salt; heat until steaming. Remove from heat. Stir in apple and vanilla; cool. Add egg and oil; stir until combined. Set aside.

③ In a small bowl stir together pecans, brown sugar, butter, 1 teaspoon flour, and cinnamon; set aside.

④ In a medium bowl whisk together the 1½ cups flour, baking powder, and baking soda. Add milk mixture all at once to flour mixture. Stir just until combined. Spoon batter into prepared baking pan. Sprinkle evenly with pecan mixture.

⑤ Bake about 25 minutes or until a knife inserted near the center comes out clean. Cool slightly. Serve warm.

PER SERVING 179 cal, 7 g fat (1 g sat. fat), 20 mg chol, 151 mg sodium, 27 g carb, 2 g fiber, 3 g pro

Stovetop Peach-Blackberry Crisp

Stovetop Peach-Blackberry Crisp

As easy as fruit crisps are to make, this stove-top version is truly a breeze and can be ready to enjoy—warm, with ice cream—in less than an hour from the time you start it.

MAKES 6 servings **START TO FINISH** 35 minutes

2	tablespoons butter
¼	cup chopped pecans
¼	cup regular rolled oats
3	tablespoons packed brown sugar
2	tablespoons sweetened shredded coconut
⅛	teaspoon ground cinnamon
4	firm, ripe peaches, pitted and sliced
1	tablespoon lemon juice
1	cup fresh blackberries
1½	cups low-fat vanilla ice cream or frozen yogurt

① For the topping, in a large nonstick skillet melt 1 tablespoon of the butter over medium heat. Stir in pecans, oats, 1 tablespoon of the brown sugar, the coconut, and cinnamon. Cook and stir for 6 to 8 minutes or until mixture begins to brown. Spread topping evenly on a baking sheet; set aside. Wipe out the skillet with a paper towel.

② In the same skillet melt the remaining 1 tablespoon butter over medium-high heat. Add peaches, the remaining 2 tablespoons brown sugar, and the lemon juice. Bring to boiling; reduce heat. Simmer, uncovered, about 5 minutes or until juices are slightly thickened. Fold in blackberries.

③ To serve, spoon about ⅔ cup of the peach mixture into each of 6 serving dishes. Sprinkle the topping over. Top with ice cream.

PER SERVING 225 cal, 10 g fat (4 g sat. fat), 13 mg chol, 61 mg sodium, 35 g carb, 6 g fiber, 4 g pro

Strawberry-Rhubarb Crisp ♥

Rhubarb appears briefly in late spring. Fans of the tart, nostalgic fruit eagerly await the pies, crisps, cakes, and sauces they will make. It is often combined with strawberries, as in this ruby-color crisp.

MAKES 6 to 8 servings **PREP** 15 minutes **BAKE** 40 minutes **COOL** 20 minutes **OVEN** 375°F

⅓	cup strawberry preserves
⅛	teaspoon ground cinnamon or nutmeg
2	cups sliced fresh strawberries
2	cups sliced fresh rhubarb
3	tablespoons all-purpose flour
½	cup quick-cooking rolled oats
2	tablespoons cornmeal
2	tablespoons honey
1	teaspoon vanilla

① Preheat oven to 375°F. In a large bowl stir together preserves and cinnamon. Add strawberries and rhubarb; stir gently to coat. Add flour; stir gently until combined. Spoon into a 9-inch pie plate. Bake, uncovered, for 20 minutes.

② Meanwhile, in a small bowl stir together rolled oats and cornmeal. Stir in honey and vanilla until combined. Sprinkle over fruit. Bake, uncovered, about 20 minutes or until topping is golden brown and fruit is tender and bubbly.

③ Cool about 20 minutes before serving. Serve warm.

PER SERVING 145 cal, 1 g fat (0 g sat. fat), 0 mg chol, 9 mg sodium, 33 g carb, 3 g fiber, 2 g pro

Peach Crisp: Prepare as above, except substitute peach or apricot preserves for the strawberry preserves and 4 cups peeled and sliced fresh peaches or sliced nectarines for the strawberries and rhubarb. Stir 2 teaspoons lemon juice into the preserves mixture before adding fruit.

Pineapple Crisp

With coconut and macadamia nuts, this unusual crisp offers up a taste of the tropics.

MAKES 6 to 8 servings **PREP** 25 minutes
BAKE 30 minutes **OVEN** 375°F

- ½ cup granulated sugar
- 1 tablespoon all-purpose flour
- 1 teaspoon ground cinnamon
- ¼ teaspoon salt
- 4 cups cubed fresh pineapple
- ½ cup dried cranberries or dried tart cherries, snipped
- 2 tablespoons lemon juice
- ½ cup packed brown sugar
- ½ cup all-purpose flour
- ½ cup rolled oats
- ¼ cup butter
- ¼ cup flaked coconut
- ¼ cup chopped macadamia nuts
  Pineapple, mango, or lemon sorbet (optional)

① Preheat oven to 375°F. Grease a 2-quart square baking dish; set aside. In a large bowl stir together granulated sugar, 1 tablespoon flour, cinnamon, and salt. Stir in pineapple, dried fruit, and lemon juice. Transfer to prepared baking dish; set aside.

② For topping, in a small bowl stir together brown sugar, ½ cup flour, and oats. Using a pastry blender, cut in butter until mixture resembles coarse crumbs. Stir in coconut and nuts. Sprinkle topping over pineapple mixture.

③ Bake for 30 to 35 minutes or until topping is golden. If desired, top each serving with sorbet. Serve warm.

PER SERVING 419 cal, 14 g fat (7 g sat. fat), 20 mg chol, 179 mg sodium, 72 g carb, 4 g fiber, 3 g pro

Apple Crisp

To prevent the apples from turning brown as you peel and slice them, toss the slices with a tiny bit of lemon juice.

MAKES 6 servings **PREP** 25 minutes
BAKE 35 minutes **OVEN** 375°F

- 6 cups sliced, peeled cooking apples
- 3 to 4 tablespoons granulated sugar
- ½ cup regular rolled oats
- ½ cup packed brown sugar
- ¼ cup all-purpose flour
- ¼ teaspoon ground cinnamon, ginger, or nutmeg
- ¼ cup butter
- ¼ cup chopped nuts or flaked coconut
  Vanilla ice cream (optional)

① Preheat oven to 375°F. In a large bowl combine apples and granulated sugar. Transfer to a 1½- to 2-quart square baking dish; set aside.

② For topping, in a medium bowl combine the oats, brown sugar, flour, and cinnamon. Cut in butter until mixture resembles coarse crumbs. Stir in the nuts. Sprinkle topping over apples.

③ Bake for 35 to 40 minutes or until apples are tender and topping is golden. If desired, serve warm with ice cream.

PER SERVING 298 cal, 12 g fat (5 g sat. fat), 20 mg chol, 60 mg sodium, 49 g carb, 3 g fiber, 3 g pro

Peach or Cherry Crisp: Prepare as above, except substitute 6 cups sliced, peeled ripe peaches or fresh pitted tart red cherries (or two 16-ounce packages frozen unsweetened peach slices or frozen unsweetened pitted tart red cherries) for the apples. For the filling, increase granulated sugar to ½ cup and add 3 tablespoons all-purpose flour. If using frozen fruit, bake for 50 to 60 minutes or until filling is bubbly across entire surface.

Apple Crisp

Peach Turnovers

Peach Turnovers

These old-fashioned fruit pastries may look time-consuming to make, but thanks to purchased puff pastry, they are easier than pie.

MAKES 4 servings **PREP** 25 minutes **BAKE** 15 minutes **OVEN** 400°F

- 2 tablespoons granulated sugar
- 1 tablespoon all-purpose flour
- ⅛ teaspoon ground cinnamon
- 1⅓ cups chopped peach or nectarine or chopped peeled apple (1 large)
- ½ of a 17.25- to 17.5-ounce package frozen puff pastry sheets (1 sheet), thawed
  Milk
  Coarse sugar (optional)
- ¾ cup powdered sugar
- 1 tablespoon butter, softened
- ½ teaspoon vanilla
  Dash salt
- 2 to 3 teaspoons milk

① Preheat oven to 400°F. Line a large baking sheet with parchment paper; set aside. In a small bowl stir together granulated sugar, flour, and cinnamon. Add peach; toss to coat.

② Unfold pastry. Cut pastry into 4 squares. Brush edges of squares with milk. For each turnover, evenly spoon peach mixture onto center of square. Fold one corner of a square over filling to opposite corner. Press edges with the tines of a fork to seal. Place turnover on prepared baking sheet. Prick tops of turnovers several times with a fork. Brush with additional milk and, if desired, sprinkle with coarse sugar.

③ Bake for 15 to 18 minutes or until puffed and golden brown. Cool slightly on baking sheet on a wire rack.

④ Meanwhile, in a small bowl stir together the powdered sugar, butter, vanilla, and salt. Add enough milk to make icing of drizzling consistency. Drizzle over warm turnovers.

PER SERVING 507 cal, 27 g fat (8 g sat. fat), 8 mg chol, 213 mg sodium, 63 g carb, 2 g fiber, 5 g pro

Peach-Berry Turnovers: Prepare as above except use 1 cup chopped peach, nectarine, or apple (1 medium) and add ⅓ cup fresh raspberries or blueberries to the filling.

Caramel Sauced Apples

Homemade caramel sauce really makes this simple fruit dessert special. You get the flavor and fun of a caramel apple on a stick without having it stick to your teeth.

MAKES 8 servings **PREP** 20 minutes **COOK** 10 minutes **STAND** 1 hour **COOL** 15 minutes

- ½ cup whipping cream
- ½ cup butter
- ¾ cup packed dark brown sugar
- 2 tablespoons light-color corn syrup
- 1 teaspoon vanilla
- 4 to 6 apples, cored and sliced
- 1 cup crushed cookies, such as biscotti, pecan shortbread, peanut butter, oatmeal, snickerdoodles, or chocolate chip (about 3 ounces)

① For caramel sauce, in a heavy medium-size saucepan combine whipping cream, butter, brown sugar, and corn syrup. Bring to boiling over medium-high heat (about 5 to 6 minutes), whisking occasionally. Reduce heat to medium. Boil gently for 3 minutes more. Stir in vanilla. Transfer sauce to a storage jar with a lid. Cool for 15 minutes. Let stand at room temperature 1 hour before serving. (Caramel sauce can be prepared and stored, covered, in the refrigerator up to 2 weeks.)

② To serve, place apple slices in individual bowls. Drizzle with caramel sauce. Top with crushed cookies.

PER SERVING 339 cal, 19 g fat (10 g sat. fat), 56 mg chol, 139 mg sodium, 42 g carb, 2 g fiber, 2 g pro

Quick Strawberry Shortcakes

A dollop of lemon curd gives these super-simple shortcakes an elegant, sweet-tart touch.

MAKES 4 servings **PREP** 10 minutes
BAKE according to package directions

- **4**   frozen unbaked buttermilk biscuits
- ⅓   cup strawberry jelly
- **1**   fresh strawberries, sliced
- ½   cup whipping cream
- ⅓   cup purchased lemon curd

① Bake biscuits according to package directions. Cool completely.

② Meanwhile, in a small saucepan heat jelly just until melted. Place berries in a bowl; add jelly and toss until mixed. Set aside. In a medium-size chilled mixing bowl beat whipping cream with an electric mixer on medium just until soft peaks form (tips curl).

③ Split biscuits horizontally. Spread biscuit bottoms with lemon curd; replace tops. Place biscuits on dessert plates. Spoon on fruit; top with whipped cream.

PER SERVING 472 cal, 22 g fat (10 g sat. fat), 61 mg chol, 619 mg sodium, 48 g carb, 5 g fiber, 5 g pro

quick tip   Ripe, in-season strawberries require very little attention to be exquisite. If you can get to a pick-your-own strawberry patch in late May or early June, you won't regret it. Look for strawberries that are red completely through—a sign that they are ripe and that their flavor has completely developed. If you know you won't eat all of your haul before they spoil, wash them and slice or quarter them. Toss with a little sugar and freeze in 2-cup portions in resealable freezer bags. Enjoy on cereal or yogurt, or baked into crisps

Peach Cobbler with Cinnamon-Swirl Biscuits

To peel peaches, drop them, one at a time, in boiling water for 30 seconds, then remove with a slotted spoon. Plunge into a bowl of ice water. Skins will slip off easily.

MAKES 6 servings **PREP** 30 minutes **BAKE** 25 minutes
OVEN 375°F

- **1**   cup all-purpose flour
- **1**   tablespoon brown sugar
- 1½   teaspoons baking powder
- ⅛   teaspoon baking soda
- ¼   teaspoon salt
- ¼   cup butter
- ⅓   cup milk
- ½   cup finely chopped walnuts
- **3**   tablespoons brown sugar
- ¼   teaspoon ground cinnamon
- **1**   tablespoon butter, melted
- ⅔   cup packed brown sugar
- **4**   teaspoons cornstarch
- ½   teaspoon finely shredded lemon peel
- **6**   cups sliced, peeled peaches or 6 cups frozen unsweetened peach slices
- ⅔   cup water

① For biscuits, in a bowl combine flour, 1 tablespoon brown sugar, baking powder, baking soda, and salt. With a pastry blender cut in ¼ cup butter until the mixture resembles coarse crumbs. Make a well in center of flour. Add milk all at once. Using a fork, stir until dough forms a ball.

② On a lightly floured surface, knead dough gently for 10 to 12 strokes. Roll or pat dough into a 12 x 6-inch rectangle. In a bowl combine walnuts, 3 tablespoons brown sugar, and cinnamon. Brush dough with the melted butter and sprinkle with nut mixture. From a short side, roll up in a spiral. Pinch seam to seal. Cut into six 1-inch slices.

③ For peach filling, in a saucepan stir together ⅔ cup brown sugar, cornstarch, and lemon peel. Add peaches and water. Cook and stir until bubbly. Carefully pour hot filling into an ungreased 2-quart rectangular baking dish.

④ Arrange biscuits, cut sides down, on hot filling. Bake about 25 minutes or until biscuits are golden. Cool slightly on a wire rack. Serve warm.

PER SERVING 439 cal, 17 g fat (7 g sat. fat), 28 mg chol, 348 mg sodium, 70 g carb, 5 g fiber, 5 g pro

Peach Cobbler with Cinnamon-Swirl Biscuits

Berries and Brownies

Berries and Brownies

This trifle-like dessert features a favorite flavor combination—chocolate and raspberries. Serve it with a fresh pot of coffee.

MAKES 12 servings **START TO FINISH** 15 minutes

- 4 cups fresh red raspberries
- 4 to 5 tablespoons sugar
- 2 teaspoons finely shredded orange peel
- 2 cups whipping cream
- ¼ cup raspberry liqueur (Chambord) (optional)
- 4 3-inch squares purchased brownies (or brownies made from a mix), cut into chunks

① Set aside 8 to 10 of the raspberries. In a large bowl combine the remaining raspberries, the sugar, and orange peel. Spoon fruit into a 1- to 1½- quart compote dish or serving bowl.

② In a chilled mixing bowl combine whipping cream and liqueur (if using); beat with chilled beaters of an electric mixer on medium until soft peaks form (tips curl). Spoon on fruit. Top the whipped cream with brownie chunks and reserved raspberries.

PER SERVING 263 cal, 19 g fat (10 g sat. fat), 69 mg chol, 63 mg sodium, 23 g carb, 5 g fiber, 3 g pro

quick tip If you don't have Chambord, a French raspberry liqueur, substitute orange liqueur—or skip the liqueur altogether.

No-Bake Cheesecake with Gingersnap Crust and Mango Puree

To prepare the mango, cut a thin slice off of the bottom of the fruit. Stand it on the flat end and cut down through the fruit on either side of the large pit. Score the fruit in a crisscross pattern and cut under it to release the cubes.

MAKES 12 servings **PREP** 35 minutes **CHILL** 3 hours

- Nonstick cooking spray
- 15 gingersnaps, crumbled
- 3 tablespoons butter, melted
- 2 tablespoons sugar
- ⅓ cup sugar
- 1 envelope unflavored gelatin
- 1 cup boiling water
- 2 8-ounce packages reduced-fat cream cheese (Neufchâtel), softened
- 1 teaspoon vanilla
- 1 medium, ripe mango, peeled, seeded, and cut up
- 1 tablespoon lime juice

① For the crust, lightly coat an 8-inch springform pan or a 9-inch pie plate with cooking spray; set aside. Place gingersnaps in a food processor. Cover and process until fine crumbs form. With the machine running, add melted butter and 2 tablespoons sugar through the opening in the lid, processing until crumbs are moistened. Transfer crumb mixture to the prepared pan. Press evenly into the bottom and 1 inch up the sides of the pan.

② In a small bowl combine ⅓ cup sugar and gelatin. Add the boiling water; stir about 5 minutes or until gelatin is dissolved.

③ For the cheesecake filling, in a large bowl combine cream cheese and vanilla; beat with an electric mixer on medium until combined. Gradually add gelatin, beating until combined. Pour filling into the crust.

④ In a food processor combine mango and lime juice; cover and process to a smooth puree. Press puree through a fine-mesh sieve; discard solids. Drizzle 3 tablespoons of the mango puree on the filling. Draw a toothpick through the puree and filling to marble. Cover; chill the cheesecake and remaining mango puree about 3 hours or until cheesecake is firm.

⑤ To serve, remove sides of the springform pan; cut cheesecake into wedges. Serve the remaining mango puree with cheesecake.

PER SERVING 202 cal, 12 g fat (7 g sat. fat), 36 mg chol, 206 mg sodium, 19 g carb, 1 g fiber, 5 g pro

Honeydew-Mojito Sherbet ♥

The Mojito, the famous Cuban rum cocktail, is infused with the flavors of lime and mint. This refreshing sherbet has the same flavors—minus the alcohol, so it can be enjoyed by anyone.

MAKES 10 servings **PREP** 25 minutes
STAND 10 minutes **FREEZE** 3 hours

¼	cup cold water
1	teaspoon finely shredded lime peel (set aside)
3	tablespoons lime juice
1	envelope unflavored gelatin
¾	cup sugar
½	cup fresh mint leaves
½	of a medium honeydew melon, peeled, seeded, and cubed (4 cups)
¼	cup low-fat Greek-style yogurt
	Fresh mint leaves (optional)

① In a small saucepan combine the cold water and lime juice; sprinkle gelatin over and let stand for 5 minutes to soften.

② Meanwhile, in a food processor or blender combine sugar, the ½ cup mint leaves, and the lime peel. Cover and process or blend until mint is finely chopped. Add cubed honeydew (half at a time if necessary) and yogurt; cover and process or blend until smooth.

③ Cook and stir gelatin over medium-low heat until gelatin is dissolved. Add gelatin to honeydew mixture; cover and process or blend for 1 minute.

④ Transfer to a 1½- to 2-quart ice cream freezer; freeze according to manufacturer's directions. To ripen, spoon into an airtight freezer container; cover and freeze for 3 to 4 hours or until firm.

⑤ To serve, let stand at room temperature for 10 minutes. If desired, garnish with additional fresh mint leaves.

PER SERVING 101 cal, 0 g fat (0 g sat. fat), 0 mg chol, 22 mg sodium, 23 g carb, 1 g fiber, 4 g pro

Banana Split Ice Cream Pie ♥

Here are all the flavors of the classic American soda-fountain treat, all wrapped up in a graham cracker crust.

MAKES 10 servings **PREP** 25 minutes **BAKE** 5 minutes
FREEZE 4 hours **OVEN** 375°F

1	purchased reduced-fat graham cracker crumb pie shell
1	egg white, lightly beaten
1½	cups low-fat or light chocolate ice cream
1½	cups low-fat or light vanilla ice cream
1	large banana, sliced
1	cup sliced fresh strawberries
2	tablespoons reduced-calorie chocolate-flavor syrup
⅔	cup frozen light whipped dessert topping, thawed (optional)

① Preheat oven to 375°F. Brush pie shell with egg white. Bake for 5 minutes. Cool on a wire rack.

② In a small chilled bowl stir chocolate ice cream with a wooden spoon just until softened. Spread chocolate ice cream in bottom of pie shell. In another small chilled bowl stir vanilla ice cream just until softened. Spread vanilla ice cream evenly over chocolate ice cream. Cover and freeze for at least 4 hours or until firm.

③ To serve, arrange banana and strawberry slices on ice cream. Drizzle with chocolate syrup. If desired, top each serving with whipped topping.

PER SERVING 167 cal, 5 g fat (2 g sat. fat), 6 mg chol, 115 mg sodium, 27 g carb, 1 g fiber, 3 g pro

Caramel-Nut
Brownies

Caramel-Nut Brownies

These ooey-gooey treats—studded with nuts and miniature chocolate chips—are the definition of sweet indulgence.

MAKES 16 bars **PREP** 15 minutes **BAKE** 20 minutes **OVEN** 350°F

½	cup butter
2	ounces unsweetened chocolate
1	cup granulated sugar
2	eggs
1	teaspoon vanilla
⅔	cup all-purpose flour
½	cup chopped pecans
½	cup miniature semisweet chocolate pieces
1	6¼-ounce package vanilla caramels
2	tablespoons milk
	Chopped pecans

① Preheat oven to 350°F. Grease a 9 x 9 x 2-inch baking pan; set aside. In a medium saucepan combine butter and chocolate; heat and stir over low heat until melted. Add granulated sugar, eggs, and vanilla. Using a wooden spoon, beat lightly just until combined. Stir in flour and ½ cup nuts.

② Spread batter in prepared pan. Sprinkle chocolate pieces on batter. Bake for 20 minutes. Cool in pan on a wire rack.

③ For the caramel topping, unwrap the vanilla caramels. In a small saucepan combine caramels and milk. Cook and stir over medium-low heat until smooth.

④ Drizzle brownies with caramel topping and sprinkle with additional chopped nuts. Cool in pan. Cut into bars.

PER BAR 143 cal, 8 g fat (2 g sat. fat), 27 mg chol, 75 mg sodium, 17 g carb, 0 g fiber, 2 g pro

Five-Layer Bars

These rich and chewy bars couldn't be any easier to make. There's no chopping or stirring. Just layer each ingredient in the pan and bake.

MAKES 30 bars **PREP** 10 minutes **BAKE** 37 minutes **OVEN** 350°F

2	13-ounce packages soft coconut macaroon cookies (32 cookies)
¾	cup sweetened condensed milk
¾	cup semisweet chocolate pieces
¾	cup raisins or dried cranberries
1	cup coarsely chopped peanuts

① Preheat oven to 350°F. Arrange cookies a greased 13 x 9 x 2-inch baking pan. Press cookies together to form a crust. Bake for 12 minutes. Drizzle crust evenly with condensed milk. Sprinkle with chocolate pieces, raisins, and peanuts. Bake for 25 minutes or until edges are light brown. Cool in pan on a wire rack. Cut into bars.

PER BAR 181 cal, 7 g fat (4 g sat. fat), 3 mg chol, 86 mg sodium, 28 g carb, 1 g fiber, 3 g pro

Five-Layer Bars

Striped Ginger Cookies ♥

Two flavors of refrigerated cookie dough makes these eye-catching cookies a snap to make. Wrap the remaining halves of dough tightly and freezer for future use.

MAKES 96 cookies **PREP** 30 minutes
BAKE 6 minutes per batch **OVEN** 375°F

- ½ of a 16½-ounce package refrigerated sugar cookie dough
- 4 tablespoons all-purpose flour
- ½ of a 16½-ounce package refrigerated gingerbread cookie dough

① Preheat oven to 375°F. In a medium bowl combine sugar cookie dough and 2 tablespoons of the flour. Using a wooden spoon, stir until well mixed. In another medium bowl combine gingerbread cookie dough and remaining flour; stir until well mixed.

② Shape each dough into 1-inch balls. For each cookie, roll 1 ball of each flavor into a 4-inch-long rope. Lay ropes side by side, then twist and roll together to make an 8-inch-long rope. Cut each rope into 6 pieces. Place pieces on an ungreased cookie sheet.

③ Bake for 6 to 8 minutes or until edges are set. Transfer cookies to a wire rack to cool.

PER COOKIES 23 cal, 1 g fat (0 g sat. fat), 1 mg chol, 19 mg sodium, 3 g carb, 0 g fiber, 0 g pro

Striped Ginger Cookies

Snickerdoodle Sandwiches

The filling for these sandwich cookies contains cream cheese, so you need to store them in a tightly sealed container in the refrigerator.

MAKES 24 sandwiches **PREP** 30 minutes
BAKE 7 minutes per batch **OVEN** 375°F

- 3 tablespoons granulated sugar
- 1½ teaspoons ground cinnamon
- 1 16½-ounce package refrigerated sugar cookie dough
- 1 8-ounce package cream cheese, softened
- 3 tablespoons honey
- 3 tablespoons snipped golden raisins or raisins (optional)

① Preheat oven to 375°F. In a small bowl combine sugar and 1 teaspoon of the cinnamon. Shape cookie dough into ¾- to 1-inch balls; roll balls in cinnamon-sugar to coat. Place balls 1 inch apart on an ungreased cookie sheet.

② Bake for 7 to 9 minutes or just until edges are firm. Transfer cookies to a wire rack to cool.

③ Meanwhile, for filling, in a medium bowl combine cream cheese, honey, and the remaining ½ teaspoon cinnamon. Beat with a wire whisk until smooth. If desired, stir in raisins.

④ Generously spread filling on the bottoms of half of the cookies. Top with remaining cookies, flat sides down, lightly pressing together.

PER SANDWICH 132 cal, 7 g fat (3 g sat. fat), 16 mg chol, 113 mg sodium, 16 g carb, 0 g fiber, 1 g pro

Chocolaty Peanut Butter Sandwich Cookies

Chocolaty Peanut Butter Sandwich Cookies

The coarse-sugar coating on these PB&C (that's peanut butter and chocolate) sandwich cookies gives them a sweet crunch when they're bitten into.

MAKES 25 sandwiches **PREP** 30 minutes **BAKE** 8 minutes
STAND 1 minute **OVEN** 375°F

- 1 **18-ounce package refrigerated chocolate chip cookie dough**
- ⅓ **cup unsweetened cocoa powder**
- 1 **cup peanut butter pieces**
- 3 **tablespoons coarse sugar**
- 1 **3-ounce package cream cheese, softened**
- ½ **cup peanut butter**
- 1 **tablespoon honey**

① Preheat oven to 375°F. Mix together cookie dough, cocoa powder, and peanut butter pieces until combined. Shape dough into ¾-inch balls. Roll balls in coarse sugar. Place balls 2 inches apart on ungreased cookie sheet. Using the bottom of a glass, flatten cookies to about ¼ inch.

② Bake for 8 to 10 minutes or until edges are firm. Cool for 1 minute on cookie sheet. Transfer to a wire rack to cool.

③ Meanwhile, for filling, combine cream cheese, peanut butter, and honey. Spread filling on bottoms of half the cookies. Top with remaining cookies, bottom sides down.

PER SANDWICH 180 cal, 10 g fat (4 g sat. fat), 9 mg chol, 76 mg sodium, 21 g carb, 1 g fiber, 3 g pro

quick tip Cocoa powder is either Dutch-process or natural. Dutch process is treated with alkali, which mellows the flavor and gives it a dark reddish-brown hue. Natural cocoa powder has a more intense chocolate flavor and is darker. Either one works fine in this recipe.

Triple Chocolate Kisses ♥

You are sure to get a kiss (or two) from the cocoa-obsessed in your life when you make these chocolatey treats.

MAKES 40 cookies **PREP** 40 minutes
BAKE 8 minutes per batch **OVEN** 375°F

- 1 **16½-ounce package refrigerated chocolate chip cookie dough**
- ⅓ **cup unsweetened cocoa powder**
- ⅔ **cup chocolate-flavor sprinkles**
- 2 **tablespoons milk**
- 40 **dark chocolate kisses, unwrapped**

① Preheat oven to 375°F. Lightly grease a cookie sheet; set aside. In a large resealable plastic bag, combine cookie dough and cocoa powder. Seal bag; knead with your hands until dough is well mixed. Remove dough from bag.

② Place chocolate sprinkles in a shallow dish or small bowl. Place milk in another shallow dish or small bowl. Shape dough into 1-inch balls. Dip balls in milk to moisten, then roll in chocolate sprinkles to coat. Place balls 2 inches apart on prepared cookie sheet.

③ Bake about 8 minutes or until edges are firm. Immediately press a chocolate kiss into the center of each cookie. Transfer cookies to a wire rack to cool.

PER COOKIE 96 cal, 5 g fat (2 g sat. fat), 4 mg chol, 34 mg sodium, 13 g carb, 1 g fiber, 1 g pro

Triple Chocolate Kisses

INDEX